Cambridge Elements ≡

Elements in Comparative Political Behavior
edited by
Raymond Duch
University of Oxford
Anja Neundorf
University of Glasgow
Randy Stevenson
Rice University

CONSPIRACY THEORIES AND THEIR BELIEVERS

A Comparative Outlook

Daniel Stockemer
University of Ottawa
Jean-Nicolas Bordeleau
University of Ottawa

CAMBRIDGE
UNIVERSITY PRESS

Shaftesbury Road, Cambridge CB2 8EA, United Kingdom

One Liberty Plaza, 20th Floor, New York, NY 10006, USA

477 Williamstown Road, Port Melbourne, VIC 3207, Australia

314–321, 3rd Floor, Plot 3, Splendor Forum, Jasola District Centre,
New Delhi – 110025, India

103 Penang Road, #05–06/07, Visioncrest Commercial, Singapore 238467

Cambridge University Press is part of Cambridge University Press & Assessment,
a department of the University of Cambridge.

We share the University's mission to contribute to society through the pursuit of
education, learning and research at the highest international levels of excellence.

www.cambridge.org
Information on this title: www.cambridge.org/9781009570824

DOI: 10.1017/9781009570794

First published 2025

A catalogue record for this publication is available from the British Library

ISBN 978-1-009-57082-4 Hardback
ISBN 978-1-009-57081-7 Paperback
ISSN 2754-6144 (online)
ISSN 2754-6136 (print)

Additional resources for this publication at www.cambridge.org/stockemer-bordeleau

Conspiracy Theories and their Believers

A Comparative Outlook

Elements in Comparative Political Behavior

DOI: 10.1017/9781009570794
First published online: February 2025

Daniel Stockemer
University of Ottawa

Jean-Nicolas Bordeleau
University of Ottawa

Author for correspondence: Jean-Nicolas Bordeleau, jbord047@uottawa.ca

Abstract: This Element leverages a comparative approach to understand how conspiracy theories and their believers differ within and across countries. Using original survey data from eight varied cases (Australia, Brazil, Canada, Germany, Lebanon, Morocco, South Africa, and the United States) the authors present specific contemporary conspiracy theories, illustrate how these theories appeal in their national context, and determine whether the characteristics of the typical conspiracy theory believer vary across setting. They first demonstrate that there is a wide range of conspiracy theories, some of which have worldwide reach, whereas others are more context specific. Then, they show that the determinants of individual conspiracism are very similar in the Western world and Brazil, but do not necessarily travel to Lebanon, Morocco and South Africa. Lastly, they summarize the main conclusions of this Element and discuss the need for greater comparative research on conspiracy theories and propose clear areas for future research.

Keywords: conspiracy theories, conspiracy beliefs, conspiracism, political beliefs, comparative politics

ISBNs: 9781009570824 (HB), 9781009570817 (PB), 9781009570794 (OC)
ISSNs: 2754-6144 (online), 2754-6136 (print)

Contents

1 Conspiracy Theories: An Introduction

1.1 Introduction

Despite the fact that former president Barack Obama released a copy of his birth certificate in April 2011 showing that he was born in Honolulu (Hawaii), 20 percent of Americans still believe that he was born outside the United States (Enders et al. 2020). Misinformation about his birthplace persists even with the former president providing ample evidence that he is a legitimate American-born citizen. This conspiracy theory, coined the Obama birther conspiracy, is not an isolated phenomenon: it is one example of the various conspiracy theories that have thrived in the United States over the past 100 years. Other examples include McCarthyism (the belief that some members of the US government are collaborating with Russian communists), the suspicion that the Central Intelligence Agency assassinated John F. Kennedy in 1963, and more recently the "Big Lie" (the conviction that the Democratic Party and the "deep state" stole the 2020 US Presidential Election) (Stockemer 2023).

While these examples are specific to the American context, conspiracy theories are not a phenomenon exclusive to the United States. Rather, they exist in every corner of the world. Some of these theories are global in nature. For instance conspiracies related to the COVID-19 pandemic (e.g., COVID-19 is a hoax, the pharmaceutical industry designed the virus in a lab, or China has deliberately produced and spread the infectious disease), climate change (e.g., climate change is a hoax and scientists touting its existence are lying), or cultural Marxism (e.g., a small group of Marxist critical theorists plot to destroy Western civilization by seizing control of important cultural institutions) have traveled to every corner of the globe (Busbridge et al. 2020). Other theories are more specific to a region and interwoven with the racial or political realities on the ground. For example, conspiracy theories related to HIV/AIDS are strong in South Africa due to the historical prevalence of HIV in the region. In some contexts, conspiracy theories target a foreign government or terrorist organization. For example, conspiracy theories in Lebanon explicitly or implicitly target Israel or Hezbollah for events that occurred in the country (e.g., the Beirut explosion). A third array of conspiracy theories is interlinked with a country's history and engages in denialism. For instance, there are some conspiracy beliefs in Germany (and elsewhere) that deny that Hitler committed suicide or which state that the Jewish population was responsible for starting World War II. Finally, a last type of conspiracy theories targets domestic political actors. Canada provides a perfect case for this final set of theories. Examples would be the theory that Pierre Poilievre (the leader of the Conservative Party) is a Russian agent sent to Canada to polarize politics or that the media are paid actors that work with Canadian prime minister Justin Trudeau.

What these conspiratorial explanations have in common is that they are based on real events, but they offer alternative, untrue, or unconfirmed narratives to these events (Douglas et al. 2019). At the core of any such theory is the belief that there are powerful people who act "in secret for their own benefit against the common good" (Uscinski 2018: 235) and "who attempt to conceal their role" in the plot (Miller et al. 2016: 825). There are many reasons for the promulgation of conspiracy theories: they can serve to delegitimize an opponent, to whitewash one's history, to hide someone's wrongdoing, or to explain an unexplained event. Whatever the motive behind their dissemination, conspiracy theories can weaken citizens' trust in the institutions of democracy, increase polarization, undermine democratic credentials, and trigger violence (Gruzd et al. 2022; Thórisdóttir et al. 2020; Vegetti and Littvay 2022).

The literature on conspiracy theories revolves around two large axes. The first axis – the supply side – looks at how these theories spread, whereas the second axis – the demand side – looks at who believes in such theories. The supply side literature illustrates that conspiracy theories diffuse through many means. For example, they spread through their inclusion in film, including in the recognized "conspiracy cinema" genre (Dorfman 1980), through television (Arnold 2008), as well as through art and music (Partridge 2018). Another prominent media to spread conspiracy theories is the internet. In fact, according to Oliver and Wood (2014), conspiracy theories are a product of mass opinion and proliferate online through echo chambers, opinion polarization, and limited content moderation.[1] Birchall and Knight (2022) slightly nuance this finding: according to them, the internet might not necessarily allow such theories to develop, but it will definitely allow them to spread more promptly once developed. Uscinski (2018) further argues that conspiracy theory websites are not easily findable for individuals who are not already following conspiracy theories; hence, they are mostly a tool for those who already believe in them or are actively seeking conspiratorial material (see also Uscinski and Parent 2014).

When it comes to the individuals who spread such theories, the literature stresses the role of public figures such as influencers or politicians as well as ordinary citizens. According to Shin et al. (2022), elites promulgating conspiracy theories can result in their amplification on mainstream news network or social media. The perfect example of this elite-based promulgation is Donald Trump and his Making America Great Again (MAGA) Republican movement.

---

[1] For instance, search engines favor and profit from popularity, not accuracy. Reddit.com is a prominent platform on which some conspiracy theories spread. The platform's anonymity and its short list of rules create the perfect environment for conspiracy theories to form and spread (Klein et al. 2019).

It is probably fair to say that COVID-19-related conspiracies such as the use of Hydroxychloroquine to cure COVID-19 (Baker and Maddox 2022) and the theory that the US election was fraudulent or stolen (Tollefson 2021) would not have received that much attention without the explicit endorsement and propagation of the former US president and other high-level politicians from the Republican Party.

The second axis – or demand side – looks at the individual correlates of conspiracy theory beliefs and distinguishes between sociodemographic, political, and psychological factors. From a sociodemographic perspective, there is some albeit not unanimous evidence that education seems to be a key factor, with more educated individuals being somewhat immune to conspiratorial thinking (Bago et al. 2022; van Prooijen 2017). Other demographic factors, such as age, gender, and place of residency, only appear to have limited influence (Goreis and Voracek 2019). When it comes to political indicators, four variables stick out: populist attitudes, religiosity, and political ideology (with political extremists especially on the right to be more likely to believe in conspiracy theories), as well as political distrust or dissatisfaction with democracy (Casara et al. 2022; Erisen et al. 2021; Schlipphak et al. 2022). Finally, in terms of psychological characteristics, research sometimes finds a positive relationship between need for closure and increased tendency to believe in conspiracy theories (Marchlewska et al. 2018; Umam et al. 2018). Lower levels of self-esteem also seem to foster conspiratorial thinking (Swami et al. 2014).

The existing research on conspiracy beliefs is still strongly US-focused (Enders et al. 2022; Uscinski 2018) and is only slowly beginning to include other cases such as Australia (Marques et al. 2022), Brazil (Santini et al. 2022), Canada (Travica 2022), and Germany (Jensen et al. 2021). Truly comparative studies are even fewer in number. One strand of these studies takes a macro-level perspective and illustrates that conspiracy beliefs are stronger in some national setting (e.g., South Africa) than in another (e.g., Chile) (see Hornsey and Pearson 2022; Hornsey et al. 2023). Another strand looks at the individual determinants of conspiracy theories and how much these are alike from one national context to another. Most notably, Walter and Drochon (2022) find that country context does not matter in determining individual beliefs in conspiracy theories. However, this study only tackles conspiracy believers in two very similar contexts, Western Europe and the United States, and might just not be generalizable across time and space. Given the few comparative studies there is some need for more of such studies to understand the degree to which the standard constituents of conspiracy theory beliefs travel from one context to another one.

1.2 The Present Research

In this Element, we aim to add on the budding comparative literature on conspiracy theory believers and further broaden the international dimension of the mainly US-centric literature. To do so, we have chosen to focus on eight cases (four Western cases and four non-Western cases). The four Western cases are Australia, Canada, Germany, and the United States; four countries that are similar in that they are long-standing Western democracies with a comparable political culture, but at the same time different in terms of socioeconomic and institutional features (including the size of the country, the party system, and electoral system). These Western countries also differ in that they all have various country-specific conspiracy theories. We add to these Western countries four emerging democracies: Brazil, Lebanon, Morocco, and South Africa. These four countries have an important history of conspiracy theories as demonstrated by the presence of several such theories (e.g., theories that target another government in the case of Lebanon and theories that are race based in the case of South Africa) (Hogg et al. 2017; Lahoud 2023).

To make a comparative contribution to the literature on conspiracy theories, this Element considers five research questions:

(1) What are main conspiracy theories in different countries?
(2) How prevalent are different conspiracy theories around the world?
(3) Who believes in various conspiracy theories?
(4) How does the typical conspiracy believer differ across contexts?
(5) Do the same factors explain beliefs in distinct conspiracy theories?

We believe that the answers to these questions will benefit the broader research agenda in two major ways. First, this research will expand our understanding of conspiracy theories in different country cases that have yet to receive much attention (especially Lebanon, Morocco, and South Africa, but also Australia, Canada, and Germany). Second, this research will provide important findings for the existing agenda, most notably about the generalizability of the extant political, sociological, and psychological literature in different contexts. In addition, this Element will help us determine if the same factors explain individuals' tendency to believe in one or more conspiracies, and if those constituents also explain conspiratorial beliefs in Western and non-Western countries. We trust that this Element will be a leap forward in a growing research enterprise focused on the intersection of context and content in the study of conspiracy theories and their believers.

1.3 Data and Methods

Not only do we aim to bridge possible differences between the Western and non-Western world but we are also interested in studying the typical conspiracy theory believer and the factors that account for someone's higher or lower likelihood to believe in such theories. To tap into recent conspiracy theories, and to explain the typical believer, we rely on the Comparative Conspiracy Research Survey (CCRS), an original survey we put in the field in the eight counties we study in December 2022 and January 2023.[2] Table 1 presents descriptive statistics for the key sociodemographic factors across our eight cases. The samples of all countries are representative of the population for age and education as well as balanced in terms of gender. However, in the cases of Lebanon, Morocco, and South Africa, the samples are not completely representative, and the mean age of respondents is below the census averages. Moreover, in Lebanon, male respondents are slightly overrepresented.

Table 1 Summary Statistics by Country

	N	Mean Age		Proportion of Men (%)		Language (s)
		Sample	Population	Sample	Population	
Australia	1,026	44.3	42.0	51.0	49.3	English
Brazil	1,024	38.7	32.4	49.0	48.5	Portuguese
Canada	999	46.7	41.7	49.0	49.1	English; French
Germany	1,027	46.9	44.6	48.0	49.5	German
Lebanon	931	30.5	29.8	68.0	50.4	Arabic
Morocco	1,072	36.2	29.1	55.0	50.3	Arabic; French
South Africa	1,016	37.1	26.9	51.0	48.9	English
United States	1,006	44.3	38.9	44.0	48.9	English

Note. Population data from Australian Bureau of Statistics (Australia); Statistics Canada (Canada); Statista (Brazil, Lebanon, Morocco, and South Africa); Statistisches Bundesamt (Germany); Census Bureau (United States).

[2] This survey was approved by the University of Ottawa Research Ethics Committee (File # S-06-21-7068).

We present a breakdown of all measures, which we use in this research, including the specific wording of each variable and scale items, in the supplementary material. Moreover, we present a more precise operationalize of our main independent variables in Section 4. Precisely, in Section 4.1.4, we display the main question wording for the various sociopolitical, psychological, and demographic factors we use in the analyses.

1.4 Outline of the Book

The Element has five sections (including this introduction). In the next section, we define conspiracy theories and discuss their historical reach. The latter part of this second section provides answers to the first research question, namely the subject and prevalence of various conspiracy theories in our eight country cases. To determine contemporary conspiracy theories in the eight countries we study, we solicited the help of eight research assistants who were tasked to comprehensively research primary (e.g., social media, web sources, etc.) and secondary sources (e.g., academic literature) for all our case studies.[3] We present and discuss the conspiracy theories which we decided to cover in Section 2.

The third section examines the extent to which conspiracy beliefs are widespread across the eight countries. To achieve this, we rely on descriptive statistics from the Comparative Conspiracy Research Survey (CCRS) (Bordeleau et al. 2023). In more detail, we present bar graphs for four to seven conspiracy theories per country, which illustrate the percent of respondents, who agree and disagree with the respective conspiracy theory.

The fourth section relies on the same dataset to tap into the factors accounting for individual variation in the likelihood that someone believes in conspiracy theories. Focusing on sociopolitical, psychological, and demographic factors, we examine whether the correlates of conspiracy theory beliefs are different between the citizens of the eight countries covered, and if so, what the source of variation is. Lastly, the fifth section provides a general discussion of our findings and presents the main contributions of our work. We conclude by laying out some potential areas for future research.

2 Definition, History, and the Conspiracy Theories We Cover

2.1 Definition

In their chapter "The History of Conspiracy Theory Research: A Review and Commentary," Butter and Knight (2019) trace the academic history of

---

[3] We made sure to assign Germany to a German-speaking student, and Lebanon to an Arabic-speaking student. For the other four countries (i.e. Australia, Canada, South Africa, and the United States), English was the main language.

conspiracy theories and their definitions back to the post–World War II period. According to the authors, conspiratorial thinking is as an irrational practice, a meaning-making cultural exercise, or an unscientific way of understanding social relations that acts as an opposition to the Enlightenment of the 1940s and 1950s. In his seminal work, Hofstadter (1966: 14) provides the first comprehensive definition of conspiracism. He characterizes conspiracy theory endorsements as beliefs in a "vast, insidious, preternaturally effective international conspiratorial network designed to perpetrate acts of most fiendish character." Contemporary definitions slightly refine Hofstadter's (1966) characterization. Most of these definitions involve the belief in a powerful covert group who is responsible for a tragic or harmful event (Byford 2011; Douglas et al. 2019). In the words of Douglas et al. (2019: 14), a conspiracy theory "attempts to explain the ultimate causes of significant social and political events and circumstances with claims of secret plots by two or more powerful actors."

All major definitions normally share the assumption that "actors, usually more powerful than the average citizen, are engaging in wide-ranging 'black-boxed' activities to which individuals can attribute an insidious explanation to a confusing event" (Miller et al. 2016: 825). Any conspiracy theory incorporates three essential elements: an explanation of a specific event, the involvement of a powerful group, and an element of secrecy (Douglas et al. 2019; Enders et al. 2020). The contemporary literature also makes the distinction between a conspiracy and a conspiracy theory clear. A conspiracy is a "secret plot by two or more powerful actors" (Keeley 2019; Pigden 2019), which refers to "a real, actual event," while conspiracy theories "refer to an accusatory perception which may or may not be true" (Uscinski 2018: 235). Many such theories view politicians as untrustworthy figures responsible for deceiving their populations into believing untrue accounts of events (Enders 2019; Siddiqui 2020). However, some conspiracy theories are also government corroborated and spread by the powerful political actors themselves (e.g., Donald Trump or Jair Bolsonaro). Importantly, the actors implicated in conspiracy theories are not always striving for political power but can instead aspire to gain social, cultural, or economic power (Gemenis 2021; Min 2021). Whatever the source or the target, conspiracy theories possess unique epistemic properties akin to systems of belief or religion (though not the same), which separates them from an ordinary set of ideas that can be easily disproven (Uscinski 2018).

2.2 The History of Conspiracism

While we are currently in a time where conspiracy theories are widespread, such theories are not a new development; they have existed for hundreds of years. They generally thrive during times of hardship and anxiety, such as during wars, economic hardship, or pandemics (Napolitano and Reuter 2023). For example, in their article on the history of conspiracy theories, Van Prooijen and Douglas (2017) discuss two interlinked conspiracy theories, which spread at the time of Emperor Nero in ancient Rome approximately 2,000 years ago. The first conspiracy theory goes as follows: during the year AD 64, there was a huge fire in Rome, during which Nero was out of town. The fire destroyed large parts of the city. According to the conspiracy theory, Nero, together with his friends, deliberately started the fire to rebuild Rome and rejoiced when Rome was burning. Upset by this conspiracy theory targeting himself, Nero started his own conspiratorial explanation according to which the Christian community was responsible to for setting Rome ablaze. Nero went on to use this conspiracy theory to crucify or burn alive many Christians (Brotherton 2015).

Other conspiracy theories have existed for hundreds of years if not more. Most notably, anti-Semite conspiracies have been a constant throughout modern history. For example, in Medieval Times, the Catholic Church and worldly dignitaries blamed Jews for bringing or spreading diseases like the plague. In more recent times, elites deliberately blamed Jews for moments of crises such as war, economic hardship, and the spread of communism (Pipes 1999). In particularly, anti-Jewish conspiracies saw great popularity in the nineteenth and twentieth centuries. For instance, in the late nineteenth century, the so-called Dreyfus Affair, in which French officials accused a Jewish-French army captain of collaborating with the Germans, promulgated anti-Semitism into French politics and society (Begley 2009). Even more consequential, anti-Jewish conspiracies served to justify the Holocaust in the mid-twentieth century (Snyder 2017).

The history of countries is frequently also interwoven with conspiracy theories. The prime example of this is the United States (US). Every major historical pillar in the country's history triggered its own conspiracy theory. For example, during the American Revolution, rebellious colonists believed that a cabal in London wanted to impose some type of slavery on the new settlers in North America, thus fostering their determination for independence. Several years later, at the start of the American Republic, in the 1790s, the then famous congregational minister, Jeddiah Morse of the Federalist Party, warned of the existence of a Bavarian Illuminati linked to Republican leader Thomas Jefferson. The goal of this secret society was supposedly to ruin Christianity in the United States (Stauffer 2006).

During the time of the American Civil War, slaveholders strongly believed that abolitionists "envenomed by hate, and impelled by lust of power and dominion, were trying to eliminate slavery by subverting the republic" (Olmsted 2019: 287). Roughly fifty years later, to justify the US's entry into the First World War, the US government including President Wilson, used conspiracy theories to quell any internal resistance to send troops to Europe. For example, Wilson himself affirmed that Germany had infiltrated the US government with spies and criminal intrigues to destroy America's national unity (Olmsted 2019). During World War II, twenty-five years later, the belief that the entire Japanese population in the West would rise and commit sabotage served as a justification for the imprisonment of more than 120,000 Japanese Americans both before and during the war (Kashima 2011).

The next important episode of American history, the post–World War II period saw the spread of McCarthyism (or the belief that some members of the United States government are collaborating with Russian communists). These unfounded allegations served as justification for political purges. As the next milestone event, the assassination of John Fitzgerald Kennedy in 1963 served as the basis for the formulation and promulgation of several conspiracy theories related to his death. The most famous one states that the Central Intelligence Agency (CIA) assassinated the former president. More recent conspiracy theories tackle the events of 9/11. Accounts stipulate that the United States had sufficient prior knowledge of the attacks to pre-emptively respond to them and thwart these attacks, but ignored them in order to serve the government's own ends in legitimizing entry into Afghanistan and eventually Iraq (Martin 2001; Martin 2002). Finally, some of the most recent contemporary theories tackle QAnon and the Big Lie. The QAnon theory emerged roughly seven years ago. In October 2017, Q made their first cryptic post on the anonymous image board website 4chan. Q later moved to 8chan to make his posts. QAnon affirms that a cabal of pedophilic elites rule the world and extract life-extending chemicals from children, and that military generals selected Donald Trump in the 2016 election to break up this cabal (Roose 2021).[4] The Big Lie, which is part of QAnon, and which former president Trump spreads himself, argues that the Democratic Party and the "deep state" stole the 2020 US presidential elections (Arceneaux and Truex 2023).

In short, conspiracism and conspiracy theories are no recent phenomena. While they have become increasingly salient in the past decade, such conspiracies have existed long before the twenty-first century. The advent of technology such as social media has facilitated their spread and allowed some of these conspiracies to reach a global audience.

---

[4] QAnon believers conceive of Donald Trump almost in a religious aspect, seeing him a "savior" against shadowy evildoers.

2.3 The Conspiracy Theories We Cover

Conspiracy theories have existed as long as human race began. Nevertheless, we are currently in an era of increased salience. Propelled by international crises, the rise of populism, and an unstable world order, conspiracy theories have propagated increasingly rapidly over the past decade. There are hundreds of conspiracy theories, which exist in different parts of the world. Some of these theories are global in nature and have spread to nearly every corner of the globe. Others are more local and restricted to a certain country or region. For inclusion into this Element, we have selected a distinct sample of conspiracies. We chose these conspiracy theories based on some in-depth contextual research conducted by our research assistants. In addition, to some local conspiracy theories, we included in our sample of such theories widespread and common conspiracy theories currently circulating around the world. These theories include several theories related to COVID-19 and one related to climate change.

The three COVID-19-related conspiracy theories are: (1) "big pharmacy orchestrated the Sars-Cov-2 and Monkeypox viruses for their own financial benefits," (2) "the pandemic is being used by elites to swap capitalism with communism," and (3) Bill Gates and George Soros are responsible for the onset of the COVID-19 pandemic. We have deliberately chosen one related to big business and one related to an existing anti-Marxism conspiracy (i.e., cultural Marxism), both of which serve as perfect target in the current (right-wing) populist global climate. The third one is more of an anti-Western or anti-Imperialist conspiracy theory, which we asked in the non-Western countries. For the climate change conspiracy theory, we have selected probably the most circulated one in the world: "climate change is a hoax, and scientists are lying about its existence." The local conspiracy theories tackle varied topics and subjects, which are representative of the local context, and in the case of Germany, we also include two niche theories tackling World War II. We recognize that our list of conspiracies is not representative of all conspiracy theories which are prominent in the world today. However, we believe that the selected conspiracy theories are diverse in their origins and subjects and thus provide a good sample.

2.3.1 Global Conspiracy Theories

Global conspiracy theories are transboundary in nature: they spread across the globe in various forms and find believers in all types of contexts. Recently, the most prominent global conspiracy theories tackle the COVID-19 pandemic. Other conspiracies with international reach relate to climate change denialism.

In this section, we introduce both types of global conspiracy (i.e., those related to COVID-19 and climate change).

COVID-19 Conspiracy Theories

In the last couple of years, the most prominent conspiracy theories in the eight countries we cover have been COVID-19-related conspiracies (Bierwiaczonek et al. 2020; Douglas 2021; Romer and Jamieson 2020). The uncertainty and anxiety brought by the pandemic created some fertile ground for such theories to develop and spread (Mari et al. 2022). The emergence of the pandemic has also allowed for speculation, as nobody knows with certainty how the virus came to be.[5] This uncertainty has opened up numerous possibilities for interpretation and has allowed conspiracy theories to spread. For example, some conspiracy theories state that the virus was human made. Versions of these conspiracies include the belief that COVID-19 was manufactured in a Chinese lab (see Bertrand et al. 2021) or that the pharmaceutical industry orchestrated the pandemic (Stecula and Pickup 2021). An alternative version explains the onset of the pandemic based on the belief that 5G waves caused the virus. The pure coincidence that Wuhan (the Chinese province where the virus was first detected) installed 5G cell phone towers in 2019 supposedly supported this claim (Heilweil 2020). Finally, a very radical conspiracy theory states that the emergence of the COVID-19 virus was a deliberate plot by Jews to expand their influence in the world. This anti-Semitic conspiracy stipulates that Israel framed China to bring them down. A component of this theory also spreads the notion that Jews profited from the pandemic through stock market volatility and the vaccine roll-out. Such anti-Jewish theories also lean to the stereotype that Jews are greedy and want to rule the world (Anti-Defamation League 2020).

Another type of COVID-19 conspiracy theories tackles the vaccine rollout and the health measures set in place to protect the population. For instance, theories that the vaccine contains trackable microchips or causes autism, infertility, or autoimmune diseases have spread in nearly every corner of the world (Stecula and Pickup 2021; Ullah et al. 2021). More radical theories, propagated by radical groups in Germany and elsewhere in Europe, have spread the idea that the COVID-19 pandemic was a "new Holocaust" and that public health measures implemented by authorities were a new level of Nazi atrocities aimed at exterminating the white population (Jeitler 2021).

A third group of theories has linked the COVID-19 pandemic to existing conspiracy theories. Most notably, they have been linked to cultural Marxism,

---

[5] The most likely scenario is that the virus was from bats and had reached humans through zoonotic transmission (Khan et al. 2020).

which stipulates the idea that a small group of Marxist theorists are using political correctness as a pretext to destroy Western civilization by coopting important state institutions such as education (Busbridge et al. 2020). With its origin in the United States in the 1990s, the initial conspiracy theory of cultural Marxism has spread from North America to the world. Most notably, terrorist Anders Behring Breivik (known as "Fjotolf Hansen") relied on cultural Marxism as a pretext to kill seventy-seven people by detonating a bomb in Oslo and by killing young Social Democrats at a mass shooting in Utøya, Norway (de Graaf et al. 2013).

In the current climate of culture wars, which supposedly rage in many Western but also non-Western countries, cultural Marxist tropes have made it into mainstream society. To illustrate, Bernardi (2015: 730) wrote in the book *The Conservative Revolution* that "cultural Marxism has been one of the most corrosive influences on society over the last century." Over the past decade, cultural Marxism has featured as a strong tool to reject progressive teaching and accommodations in school for intersex, gender diverse, transgender, and queer students (Thompson 2019). For example, Australian Liberal Member of Parliament (MP) George Christensen compares gender-affirmative programs in school to a pedophile grooming a child (Alcorn 2016). Because it fits the climate of the time, cultural Marxism has also become one of the most widely distributed conspiracy theories during the COVID-19 pandemic. The theory argues that progressive or Marxist actors have orchestrated the pandemic to take away individual freedoms and to impose their Marxist ideology on society with the final aim of creating a worldwide Marxist revolution.

COVID-19 conspiracies of different types have spread in the eight countries we cover. In Western contexts (i.e., Australia, Canada, Germany, and the United States), a feeling of exasperation with the health measures nurtured by economic troubles, social isolation, and the sentiment that the restrictions implemented by the various government took away fundamental freedoms cultivated the radicalization of parts of the citizenry and pushed many to resort to conspiracy theories (Davies et al. 2023). The prime example of this mobilization was the Freedom Convoy in Canada, a movement that, by occupying the streets around Parliament, paralyzed the Canadian capital Ottawa for over three weeks in February 2022 (Gillies et al. 2023). What started as a small movement run by truckers merged into a mass-movement which at its height was supported by 30 percent of the Canadian population (Leger 2022). At the core of the movement were several conspiracy theories featuring not only the onset of the pandemic and the roll out of the vaccine but also more general topics in the conspiracy genre. Major themes included: COVID-19 was an intentionally manufactured and spread virus; the world's leaders used the pandemic as a pretext to install a totalitarian world government that would control all aspects of the economy and society; Vladimir Putin is a hero who fights against the Deep State; and the Big Lie, or the belief that the American Election was stolen (Farokhi 2022). In fact, the adherence to several of these conspiracy theories helped participants shape a common identity that allowed them to define themselves and to delegitimize others including governments or elites (Konopka 2023).

In the four non-Western countries we study (i.e., Brazil, Lebanon, Morocco, and South Africa), high levels of suspicion about the hegemony of Western medicine (including vaccines) and skepticism regarding the "true" origins of the pandemic nurtured conspiratorial thinking. For instance, in South Africa, there were large amounts of mis- and disinformation about the virus' origins spreading online and in chat group networks. This disinformation mostly tackled the "sinister motives of superpowers and wealthy businessmen" (Mare and Munoriyarwa 2022: 69). In, Lebanon one of the other non-Western countries we cover, many people suspected that the government used the virus to control the population (Muro 2021). The slow vaccine roll-out and its inadequate management across the country gave further legitimacy to COVID-19 conspiracy theories. In fact, 40 percent of the vaccination sites in Lebanon did not have proper site management and some sites did not inform the public of the possible side effects of the vaccine (Lewis 2021). This lack of transparency in the vaccine roll-out severely contributed to citizens' hesitancy to see the pandemic as it was: the largest pandemic in decades. Instead, it led many to seek alternative explanations in the form of conspiracy theories. To support this claim, Ghaddar et al. (2022) report that, in 2021, over 60 percent of the population fully or somewhat believed in some misinformation related to COVID-19.

In Morocco religious interpretations of the pandemic took center stage. For example, in a survey realized by Chaara (2021) more than two-thirds of participants either fully or partially adhered to the idea that the virus was a divine punishment linked to the legalization of alcohol in holy places and of homosexuality in many places around the world. Similarly to Lebanon, a high percentage of citizens believed that the virus was manipulated either for commercial purposes or to control the population, and that either the United States or China had a role in its spread (Zag and Mifdal 2024). In South Africa, a history of pandemic-related misinformation and deep distrust in Western medicine created some fertile ground for COVID-19-related conspiracies to spread on the African Horn (Steenberg et al. 2023).

In Brazil, the final non-Western country we study, COVID-19 conspiracies took the center stage because the president at the time, Jair Bolsonaro, maintained a consistent approach of denial. On multiple occasions, the former president declared that the virus was a fantasy, participated in demonstrations and events directed against the lockdown measures imposed by (some) governors in (some) of the federal states, advocated the use of Chloroquine to treat COVID-19 patients, and questioned the efficacy of vaccines (Burni et al. 2023). In the highly polarized Brazilian population many Bolsonaro supporters followed their leader and either minimized or outright denied the existence of the virus (Farias et al. 2022). Over the two years, the pandemic took center stage in Brazilian politics; (mis)information and interpretation battles raged in the country between supporters of Bolsonaro and opponents concerning the existence and severity of the pandemic, and several COVID-19-related conspiracies spread in the country (Ramos et al. 2022). A prominent version that Bolsonaro spread himself was the connection of the pandemic to cultural Marxism (Farias et al. 2022).

Because of the dominance of pandemic-related conspiracies over the past couple of years, we have chosen to study several of such theories depending on the prevalence of a given theory in a given country context. The first one is the cultural Marxist COVID-19 conspiracy theory which states that the pandemic was used by elites to swap capitalism with communism. Because of the global nature of this conspiracy theory, we used it in all eight countries we study. In context, we found the spread of the second and third conspiracy theories we use more context specific. In six of the eight countries (i.e., Australia, Canada, Morocco, Germany, South African, and the United States) we asked respondents the rather general theory, whether they believe that big pharma orchestrated the Sars-Cov-2 and Monkeypox viruses for their own financial benefit. In Lebanon, the absence of a large profit-driven pharmaceutical industry pushed us to not ask this theory in this North African country. In Brazil, we did not ask about this theory, as well, because we did not find empirical evidence for the widespread nature of this theory.

In the four non-Western countries (i.e., Brazil, Lebanon, Morocco, and South Africa) we added a third COVID-19-related conspiracy theory, according to which Bill Gates and George Soros are responsible for the onset of the pandemic. We find it important to ask this conspiracy theory that defies Western hegemony in these four countries. For decades, the relationship between any of these emerging countries and the West has been sour (Hancock 1998). This suspicion is rooted not only in colonialism and Western imperialism but also in more contemporary social or political factors. For example, in Morocco and Lebanon there is a deep suspicion toward the West rooted in Muslim religiosity and dogmatism (Albaghli and Carlucci 2021). The heterogeneity of the Lebanese and Moroccan society and the West's strong support for Israel have further engrained anti-Western sentiment directed particularly against the

United States (Abadi 2020). Particularly, in Lebanon, this influence might have been exacerbated by the strong impact of Hezbollah in the country and its ties to Syria (Levitt 2024).

In South Africa, Apartheid and huge income disparities have left deep wounds in society – wounds that up to this day nurture prejudice and negative opinions against the (former) oppressors (Adam and Moodley 2023). And in Brazil, there is latent suspicion toward Western, and particularly US, hegemony, which, in part, is derived from Brazil's own global and regional aspirations,[6] which sometimes runs counter to Western interests.

We believe that, particularly in the context of a pandemic, such deep suspicion could manifest itself in a form of scapegoating of Western hegemony. More specifically, the figureheads of Western economic power – Bill Gates and George Soros – are perfect targets for conspiracies in Brazil, Lebanon, Morocco, and South Africa; they are targets that fit with pre-existing beliefs and that therefore might gain traction in the four respective populations.

Climate Change

The second type of conspiracy theory that was present across our eight country cases is the idea that climate change is a hoax. There is overwhelming consensus among the scientific community that human-made carbon emissions have contributed to the warming of the Earth with devastating consequences for the environment. These include the melting of glaciers, the rise of sea levels, and more severe weather patterns such as storms, heat waves, and draughts (Drake 2014; Harvey 2018). Despite the strong scientific evidence in support of the existence of climate change, conspiracy theories and people denying its existence have been around for the past twenty to thirty years. Among others, these conspiracies have been nurtured by Bill Gray, a professor at Colorado State University, who claimed that the heating up of the planet follows a natural circle; once this circle comes to an end, the Earth will cool again. Despite many refutations of this thesis, the claim that climate change is unreal has remained popular, especially in far right-wing circles (Douglas and Sutton 2015).

In recent years, many prominent politicians have denied the existence of climate change. For instance, US senator James Inhofe's (2012) book *The Greatest Hoax: How the Global Warming Conspiracy Threatens Your Future* outright rejects the idea that climate change exists. More recently, President Trump has repeatedly labeled reports about climate change as "politically motivated" and has recurrently argued that the United States bears no

---

[6] For example, the country has avoided to join the Western alliance in important geopolitical conflicts such as the War in Ukraine (Marcondes & de Almeida 2023).

responsibility for the increase in world temperature. He has even gone as far as mocking climate change and environmental activists. For instance, in December 2017, when the United States was hit by a severe cold front, he wrote on Twitter: "could use a little bit of that good old Global Warming that our Country, but not other countries, was going to pay TRILLIONS OF DOLLARS to protect against" (McGowan and Walters 2017).

While we expect climate change denialism to be particularly strong in the United States – research reports that up to 25 percent of the US population could be skeptical about climate change (see Sarathchandra and Haltinner 2021) – we assume the rejection of climate change to be a major conspiracy theory in all the countries we study. For example, the prominent right-wing Australian newspaper *The Spectator* regularly touts ideas that refute the existence of climate change (Meade 2020). In Germany, climate change conspiracies are a main topic in "alternative" online forums (Brüggemann et al. 2020). Canada has its own distinct climate change-related conspiracies. These conspiracies are related to federal policies toward Alberta and entertain the idea that liberals and environmental actors are working together to destroy Alberta's oil sands for their financial benefit, and that the Trudeau government is working to eliminate Alberta's oil and gas industry (Hislop 2021; Ling 2021). In Lebanon, Morocco, and South Africa, many citizens (in particular religious citizens) view climate change as a Western hoax or a plot to undermine developing countries (Bell 2011; Mazaheri 2024). In Brazil, climate change denialism took center stage during the Bolsonaro administration. Among others, the Bolsonaro government used misinformation about climate change and the importance of the protection of the rainforest as the lung of the world to justify some erratic environmental policies such as the accelerated deforestation of parts of the Amazon rainforest (Silva 2022). To encapsulate climate change denialism, we include the following conspiratorial statement in our research: climate change is a hoax, and scientists are lying about its existence.

2.3.2 Conspiracy Theories in the Eight Countries

On the pages to follow, we give a short introduction to the dominant conspiracy theories in each country. In some of the cases we study such as Brazil or Morocco, it is the global conspiracy theories that are center stage. In these places, these global conspiracy theories are interwoven with the local fabric of the country. In other countries such as Australia or the United States, there exist several country-specific conspiracy theories that reflect the cultural, economic, or societal background of a country. These conspiracy theories also often refer to the history of a country. In what follows, we give a snapshot of the dominant conspiracy theories in any of the eight cases. In cases, where such local conspiracies exist, we mainly present those. In other cases, we explain how the more general conspiracies surrounding COVID-19 and climate change denialism are salient in the local context.

Australia

Australia is an interesting case. On the one hand, all international conspiracies related to COVID-19 or the global warming of the planet are present in this country in the Southern hemisphere. In addition, we find some unique Australian conspiracies (e.g., the disappearance of Prime Minister Holt) and some with links to larger global conspiracy theories but developed their own variant (i.e., an Australian variant of QAnon).

A uniquely prominent Australian conspiracy theory relates to the disappearance of Australian prime minister Harold Holt. On December 17, 1967, Holt disappeared while swimming at Cheviot Beach, Victoria. While his death was most likely caused by accidental drowning, it spawned many conspiracy theories. Most of these claims involve a cover-up by a foreign government (Marques et al. 2022). One story stipulates that the American government assassinated Holt because he was planning to withdraw the Australian military from the war in Vietnam. The most prominent theory is that Holt was a Chinese spy who faked his death to defect to China. According to this latter conspiracy, a Chinese submarine would have taken him during his swim (Frame 2005).

Another conspiracy theory is a distinct Australian variant of QAnon. The QAnon conspiracy theory, which originated in the United States from a set of fabricated claims made by Q, an anonymous individual who affirms to be a high-level American government official has the following core message: a group of cannibalistic, Satanic pedophiles are actively working against the Trump administration. Donald Trump is fighting this group of Satan-worshiping child molesters (Bloom and Moskalenko 2022). QAnon emerged in Australia in 2018 on the social media platform Facebook (now known as Meta). It triggered moral outrage, which, in turn, contributed to the theory's spread to vast audiences across the country. Between October 2017 and June 2018, the first nine months of the theory, Australians shared more than 105,000 QAnon-related tweets. However, it was not until the pandemic that the conspiracy theory's prevalence grew (Badham 2021). The rolling lockdowns in 2020 and 2021 created an environment in which QAnon spread online. The theory has provided people with a sense of community and belonging (Badham 2021) that has spread to the nonvirtual world. There is a lot of merchandise that is available to self-identify as a believer (Zadrozny and Collins 2018). People put catchphrases such as "Where We Go One We Go All" in their social media bios to find fellow believers (Zhang et al. 2022). Thanks to its cross-pollination with other conspiracy theories, QAnon has become mainstream. Just to name a few, the theory has merged with anti-vaccination, anti-lockdown, anti-migration, anti-Semitic, and anti-5G conspiracies (Badham 2021).

As a final conspiracy theory for Australia, we add the theory according to which secret powers like the CIA or billionaire families control the world. While this is a global conspiracy theory, we have included it nevertheless given that our research of the country found it to be widespread (Halafoff et al. 2022). More generally, research has repeatedly mentioned that multiple tenets of international conspiracies flourish in Australia (Zihiri et al. 2022). Conspiratorial communities are prospering in Australia and their members often do directly identify "as patriots charged with protecting the nation" (Jones 2023). For such patriots, the more nebulous conspiracy about secret forces controlling the world, including Australia, is a perfect meta-theory to believe in. We therefore asked it alongside the COVID-19 conspiracy theories and the climate change denialism one.

Brazil

Brazil underwent polarizing and politically dramatic changes and events from 2018 to 2023, with the back-to-back elections of far-right Bolsonaro to the far-left Lula. Within this time frame, there were also coup and murder attempts, a pandemic, and other conspiracy-inducing events (Pacheco 2024). Most of the conspiracies that have taken center stage over the past years are global conspiracies. However, they are deeply embedded in the cultural, political, and social realities of the country (Santini et al. 2022). In what follows, we explain how the global pandemic-related conspiracy theories, and the climate change one fit the local fabric of the country. We also present one home-made conspiracy theory: the theory that Bolsonaro won the 2022 election.

A deeply rooted anti-imperialist and anti-globalist stance has nurtured conspiratorial thinking in Brazil for the past decades. Globalist conspiracy theories in Brazil attribute the fault of the shortcomings [of globalization] to "occult and mischievous forces secretly operating behind the façade of a profoundly globalized and multipolar international system" (de Mello and Estre 2023: 134). According to Santini et al. (2022) many Brazilians "embrace conspiratorial narratives when theorizing the geopolitical marginality of their nation as a means to make sense of covert imperialist strategies of domination." Throughout the country's history, there has been a promulgation of conspiracies with anti-imperialist/anti-US sentiment. One example of this is a conspiracy which decries the US sabotage and influence on Brazil's spaceport, largely through the US's Americanized version of racial integration being transplanted to race relations in Brazil to purposefully upset the state (Mitchell 2018). This conspiracy was widespread around one decade ago but lost its influence in recent years.

During the Bolsonaro era, globalism was not just a political strategy to persuade voters but a worldview embedded in Bolsonaro's far-right vision (de Sá Guimarães et al. 2023). In addition to globalism, nationalism and the rejection of leftish ideologies took center stage in contemporary conspiracy theorizing. Some of these conspiracy theories also include a narrative image of Jair Bolsonaro as a hero, protective savior, or messiah who is seeking to sever these corrupt globalist ties fighting for the position of Christianity in the country against the globalist, anti-nationalist forces (Demuru 2020). The two globalist conspiracy theories – (1) Bill Gates and George Soros are responsible of the onset of the Covid-19 pandemic, and (2) the pandemic is being used by a small group of elites to swap capitalism for communism in liberal democracies – perfectly fit Bolsonaro's worldview and have become center stage. The former fits into a history of conspiracies which decry George Soros as a key leader in this globalist invasion network (Santini et al. 2022). The latter has been a tool by the Brazilian (far-)right to prove that international leftist forces were conniving against Bolsonaro and his government (Soares et al. 2021).

Both theories have further served to heighten political polarization by "offering 'alternative' stories [about COVID-19] to support his [Bolsonaro's] discourse" (Soares et al. 2021: 9). They have also been a "reactionary imagination" reply/movement to the public health crisis that has allowed blame to be put on a variety of (often globally connected) groups (from leftists, to politicians, to journalists) with the aim of getting a variety of outcomes, including disinformation and removing liberty from the people (Szwako 2023).

Stemming from Bolsonaro's ascent to power, there has also been a rise in anti-environmentalist claims backed by (far-)right-wing politicians and media outlets. An example of this would be the conservative outlet *Brasil Paralelo*, a popular YouTube channel promoting anti-environmental material and environmental conspiracies, including the idea that climate change is a hoax. More broadly, Bolsonaro and his allies used the anti-environmental agenda to navigate "land use interests and to steer imperialist fears related to the use of resources by international groups" (Salles et al. 2023: 3). Nevertheless, and despite Bolsonaro and his cronies advocating climate change conspiracies, these conspiracy theories are not as widespread as other conspiracies, particularly the globalist conspiracies surrounding the pandemic (Robinson 2021).

The final conspiracy theory that we tackle is the Brazilian version of the Big Lie, or the idea that President Bolsonaro did not lose the October 2022 presidential election. Following Trump's playbook, Bolsonaro discredited the electoral system as rigged and fraudulent even before the election. In the aftermath of the election, he never officially conceded and allegedly proposed a coup plan to overthrow the legitimately elected government to some of the military's commanders. This misinformation coupled with hyper polarization and strong (social media) ties among his supporters led a group of "patriots" to ransack government buildings in the nation's capital Brasilia (and elsewhere in Brazil), nearly exactly two years after the Storm of the Capitol in the United States (Ozawa et al. 2024). The aim of this insurrection was the fostering of a military coup. While this coup attempt failed, the idea that Bolsonaro won the election remains an important trope in far-right networks, especially among the former president's ardent supporters (Bastos and Recuero 2023).

Canada

Contrary to Brazil, which, aside from the Brazilian version of the Big Lie, mainly sees the spread of global conspiracies embedded in the national context, Canada is a specific case with distinctive local conspiracies. Such local conspiracies primarily serve the purpose of attacking tools against political adversaries (see Foster and Wolfson 2010; Pennycook et al. 2022). Two rather prominent cases are: (1) Liberal media are paid actors working for Justin Trudeau, and (2) Pierre Poilievre is a Russian Agent sent to Canada to polarize politics. A third genre is local adaptations of international conspiracies. For example, the conspiracy theory that states that Liberals and environmental actors are working together to destroy Alberta's oil sands is a local version of the climate change denial conspiracy theory.

Nurtured by feelings of alienation from news reporting in the country, one important conspiracy theory emerging from the political right is the theory according to which legacy media in Canada are paid actors working for Prime Minister Justin Trudeau (Levant 2021). This conspiracy theory has been nurtured by public perceptions that Prime Minister Trudeau was a media darling, especially at the beginning of this tenure. According to this theory, Trudeau used his media influence to buy off several of the main media outlets in Canada to ensure that they would not be too critical of him and his government (Fildebrandt 2020). This conspiracy theory most notably gained traction after several right-wing influencers used a joke made by Trudeau about "paying the media" as support for their conspiratorial claims (Reuters 2022).

Among Conservatives and right-wing circles, another conspiracy theory that has emerged and targeted the prime minister and various liberal interest groups argues that Liberals secretly collaborate with environmental actors to destroy Alberta's oil sands. According to the theory, environmental actors are "in bed" with the prime minister in an attempt to destroy the oil and gas industry of the Western provinces (Murphy 2023). This conspiracy is reinforced by several right-wing actors' reliance on conspiratorial rhetoric directly linked to the Great Reset theory, which stipulates that a global elite, which the Liberals are part off, is trying to dismantle capitalism to enforce radical social change. Part of the proposed changes is the dismantling of all fossil energy sources, which includes oil sands (Djuric 2023).

Trudeau has not been the only target of conspiracy theories in Canada. Pierre Poilievre, leader of the Conservative Party, is the main protagonist in a new wave of conspiratorial talk. Indeed, some online users have begun making the case that Poilievre is in fact a foreign asset working on behalf of Russia. The headline of the known left-wing media website *Crier Media* – "What are the chances Pierre Poilievre is a foreign asset? Pretty good, actually . . ." (Blundell 2023) – amplified this sentiment. Many accounts on the social media platform X (formerly Twitter) spread this conspiracy theory. For example, users have speculated that because of his Russian agency, Poilievre cannot get a security clearance (after Poilievre refused to obtain a security clearance). They further assume that Russian funds helped him access the Conservative leadership. Others speculate that he was a secret organizer of the Freedom Convoy, which some also believed received funds from Russia.

Germany

Germany is an interesting case when it comes to conspiracy theories. In addition to the broad international conspiracies, it has its own "home-made" conspiracy theories which are sometimes also influenced by global conspiracy theories. Most notably, we can interpret the theory as the German version of QAnon, according to which NATO Operations in Germany were an attempt by Trump to liberate the country from Angela Merkel. Two more home-made conspiracies refer to World War II. The first one outright argues that Jews are responsible for the onset of World War II and the second one postulates that Hitler lived after 1945 into old age. For sure, these latter conspiracies are niche theories, but they are nevertheless important considering that they have been around for over seventy-five years.

In its original version, QAnon affirms that a secret society is in control of all politics in the United States; this secret society rigs elections, runs a sex trafficking ring, engages in pedophilia, and entertains a satanic cult in which members regularly drink the blood of children (Garry et al. 2021). The theory sees Donald Trump as a savior, who rescues America from these dark forces. In recent years, an adapted version of this conspiracy theory has begun circulating in Germany. According to this adaptation, the Federal Republic of Germany (FRG) is not an independent state. Rather, Germany is governed by the same evil forces that govern the United States, with most Germans being the employees of Angela Merkel, the "branch manager" of said company (Önnerfors and Krouwel 2021: 100). Instead of saving the United States from a dark cult, Donald Trump is supposedly saving the German population from Angela Merkel and its ill-spirited corrupt government. This theory gained traction when US soldiers were doing NATO maneuvers in Germany in 2018 and 2019. German followers of QAnon began posting videos theorizing that the training exercises were a secret operation by President Trump to liberate Germany from Chancellor Angela Merkel's government and the secret forces behind it (Bennhold 2020).

Apart from QAnon-inspired conspiracies, several theories concerning World War II and Nazi Germany have been circulating among far-right German groups over the past decades. In particular, so-called Reich Citizens – a fringe group – that rejects the existence of the German Federal Republic are very instrumental in their propagation of far-right theories. Two different types of Reich citizens exist, and each type differs in their ideological backgrounds. Reactionary Reich citizens tend to be nationalistic and desire a pre-1945 Germany; they want to achieve an "old European order untouched by modernisation processes" (Önnerfors and Krouwel 2021: 120). These Reich Citizens view themselves as being colonized by foreign powers and speak of themselves as indigenous peoples. On the contrary, individualistic Reich citizens do not want to go back to an "old Germany" but rather focus on freeing themselves from any foreign state domination (Rathje 2021). Among these Reich Citizens, several conspiracies question that Germany lost World War II, some of which even affirm that the third Reich never collapsed following World War II. Therefore, believers argue that the Nazi regime continues to exist today. Other conspiracies propagate the idea that since only an armistice took place, Germany is technically still at war (Evans 2020; Winston 2021).

We decided to include in our survey two very radical theories from the repertoire of conspiracies promulgated by Reich Citizens. The first one stipulates that Jews are responsible for the onset of World War II, and the second one argues that Hitler lived beyond 1945 and into old age. We included these two conspiracy theories not because we expect them to have the most followers but because they are some of the most abstruse and radical conspiracy theories we encountered. It will be interesting to see who believes in such theories and how the typical believer in these obscure theories differs from believers in more "mainstream" theories such as COVID-19-related theories.

Lebanon

From many ankles, Lebanon is an interesting case to study conspiracy theories. The multicultural nature of the country, with Muslims and Christian living side by side, the existence of the terror group Hezbollah, which has created a state within the state, and the country's geopolitical situation bordering Israel and Syria make it an interesting case to study conspiracy theories. In addition to the spread of international conspiracy theories, the political and social fabric of the country render it conducive for the spread of domestic conspiracy theories, which either attack Israel or Hezbollah, the militant and terrorist organization, which, de facto, controls much of the country. In addition to international global conspiracy theories, we present two home-made conspiracy theories, one that targets Hezbollah and one that targets Israel.

The first conspiracy theory results from the death of the former prime minister of Lebanon Rafic Hariri. An explosion tragically killed him, his bodyguards, and the former minister of economy in the capital in February 2005 while they were circulating in the streets of Beirut. The former prime minister was well-known for his anti-Syrian policy positions, his neoliberal attitudes, and his opposition to Hezbollah (Baumann 2016). Despite the fact that a UN investigation failed to link the assassination to high-profile individuals in Hezbollah, many Lebanese believe that the assassination took place to overturn a government wanting to cut ties with the Assad regime in Syria (Sullivan 2014). According to the conspiracy, Hezbollah had to eliminate the prime minister to access power and to put in place their Shiite government focused on issues that benefit their agenda (such as anti-Zionism).

The second conspiracy theory we cover is linked to the Beirut explosion that happened in the city's port in August 2020. According to the official investigation, the event was an accident caused by ammonite nitrate, a highly flammable material. What initially started as a fire developed into an explosion when it got in contact with the substance (Forensic Architecture 2020). Citizens of Beirut could see a big mushroom-like cloud, which resembled a nuclear weapon explosion in the aftermath of the explosion (Washington Post 2020). Leaders around the world reacted to the explosion and stirred conspiracy theories. Most notably, Donald Trump commented on the event, stating, "it looked like a terrible attack" (Spring 2020). Not only were his words later deformed and spread on platforms such as Telegram or WhatsApp but they also nurtured the conspiracy theory that sees the explosion as the direct result of the Israeli government trying to destroy a nuclear bomb stored by Hezbollah in the port.

Despite the fact that the Lebanese government, the Israeli government, and the Pentagon all declined these allegations, this conspiracy theory is a very popular explanation for the Beirut attack up to this day (El Hajj 2021). In the survey, we asked two questions related to the Beirut explosion. The first one directly asked survey respondents if they think that the Israeli government had something to do with the Beirut explosion, and the second one is more subtle and asked whether they believe that the Beirut explosion was not an accident. Since very few survey respondents wanted to answer the first question in our survey (perhaps for fear of repercussions), we relied on the second question.

Morocco

Out of the eight countries we study, Morocco is the country where we could collect the least information on existing contemporary conspiracy theories. What we found is that the history of conspiracy theories goes back to colonial times. The British occupation nurtured a feeling of deep distrust with government among the population. For example, during the colonial rule, many Moroccans believed that Great Britain and its Intelligence Service were conspiring to use and manipulate nationalist movements to maintain dominance over Morocco, the Strait of Gibraltar, and North Africa as a whole (Roslington 2014). More generally, colonial rule left a strong mark on many Moroccans, enabling prevailing imaginaries of mistrust to spread within the social and epistemological infrastructures of everyday life (Carey 2017). General feelings of distrust with authorities nurtured the spread of banal conspiracy theories, which, among others, affirm that Jews killed Princess Diana, or that Western countries fund the Islamic State of Iraq and the Levant (ISIL) with the aim of destabilizing the region and lower the oil prices (Proudfoot 2022).

Over the past two decades, anti-colonialism and engrained anti-imperialism, and suspicion of the government and a bloated bureaucracy have led to the view that the state, by conspiring with international actors, tries to forcefully shape citizens' lives (Carey 2017). In such an environment, conspiracy theories have it quite easy to spread, especially during times of crisis. This was especially the case during the outbreak of the swine flu (H1N1) virus in 2009. Some of the conspiracy theories at the time stated that the vaccine had no effect but rather was a tool to enrich the government and pharmaceutical companies. Others saw in the vaccine a deliberate attack on Arabs. Such more specific theories stated that "the vaccine was imposed on Arabs because of the financial crisis that hit the US and Europe" or "an attempt by Americans to harm Muslims" (Lohiniva et al. 2014: 3).

More recently, many versions of "truth" emerged during the COVID-19 pandemic in Morocco. One central reason for the spread of COVID-19-related conspiracies was mistrust and resistance to the government and its restrictive social control. According to Mifdal (2023: 162), anti-COVID-19 conspiracy theories spread in opposition to the "simplified truth propagated by a dominant narrative" of the Moroccan state/government/health officials. The pandemic also triggered a strong "counter-hegemonic" (p. 181) push against the government and elites, thought to be self-serving and having ulterior motives behind the pandemic restrictions. The outcome of this counter-hegemonic narrative was "total rejection of the state's policies implemented to manage the situation" (Mifdal 2023), especially the vaccine.

Because COVID-19 conspiracies took center stage in Morocco, we expect our three COVID-19-related theories to have widespread backing in the country. We also expect the climate change conspiracy theory to find some followers. The same social setup with low trust in government, and strong anti-imperialism that has pushed the spread of pandemic related conspiracies, should also serve as strong justification for the thesis that climate change is fictitious and not real.

South Africa

South Africa is another very interesting case to study conspiracy theory beliefs. As the African regional power, the country sees the spread of international conspiracy theories including the COVID-19 ones and the climate change ones. As a post-Apartheid country, it is also in a unique situation. The majority Black population remains skeptical of "white" medicine and science. Combined with the high HIV prevalence rate, which touches roughly one in five adults, this skepticism provides a fertile ground for the spread of medical conspiracy theories. Because such medical or health-related conspiracy theories are a rather unique feature of this South African country, we present three of such theories, two in relations to HIV/AIDS and one related to birth control.

Considering that South Africa is among the countries with the highest rates of adult HIV prevalence in the world – with 7.5 million adults between the ages of fifteen and forty-nine estimated to be living with HIV (UNAIDS 2022) – conspiracy theories about HIV/AIDS have been numerous. Within the category of HIV/AIDS conspiracy theories, there are several sub-beliefs including the belief that a cure for HIV/AIDS is deliberately being withheld by white scientists or that doctors have created and/or are actively injecting HIV into Black patients (Dickinson 2013). Other conspiracy theories affirm that HIV/AIDS was invented to kill Black people (Grebe and Nattrass 2012) or that HIV was invented in a laboratory (Nattrass 2012: 115).

In part, these conspiracy theories gained widespread traction because they received government support (Calfano 2020: 64). Most infamously, Thabo Mbeki (South Africa's second president in the post-Apartheid era) played a pivotal role in promoting what is described as "AIDS denialism" (Grebe and Nattrass 2012). In the early 2000s, Mbeki, together with his health minister Manto Tshabalala-Msimang, questioned the origins of HIV/AIDS in addition to arguing that HIV was not dangerous and did not lead to AIDS. He also argued that pharmaceutical medication to treat HIV/AIDS – antiretrovirals – would do more harm than good and could even lead to death (Fassin 2007).

The specific method of propagation of these views was threefold. First, Mbeki laid out the government's new position on antiretrovirals in televised speeches in 1999 and 2000, employing a rather populist discourse by criticizing Western countries' imposition of 'intellectual terrorism' on Africans who questioned the efficacy and safety of antiretrovirals. Second, Health Minister Tshabalala-Msimang, a popular minister with a high public profile at the time, controversially circulated extracts of a book by Milton William Cooper, an American who argued that AIDS was a bioweapon conjointly conceived by Jews, aliens, and the American government. Third, Mbeki's speeches and Tshabalala-Msimang's controversies created a national discussion whereby new and even more radical opinions formed and whereby new conspiracy theories emerged (Fassin 2007; Hogg et al. 2017).

Interestingly, the internet played only a minor role in spreading HIV/AIDS conspiracy theories. At first, these theories spread entirely though print and television mainstream media coverage. Only later were these theories propagated through the internet. As of 2024, HIV/AIDS conspiracy theories are still very widespread. They disseminate via multiple channels including the internet, chat groups, among friends, and through the print media (Mare and Munoriyarwa 2022). For this study, we have picked two contemporary and widespread HIV/AIDS conspiracies: (1) AIDS was created by white people to kill Black people, and (2) the government and scientists have a cure for HIV/AIDS, but they are hiding it.

Beyond HIV/AIDS, there are few other conspiracy theories that target white scientists, businesses, foreign governments, or big pharma (Fassin 2007). Several discoveries in the post-Apartheid era have nurtured such conspiracy theories. For example, such theories often cite the policies of Dr. Wouter Basson, a white scientist during the Apartheid era who conducted studies into how biological weapons could be used to further racial segregation and control (Dickinson 2013: 124). They also refer to long-standing attempts by the apartheid government to manage and limit the procreation of African children. Combined with lingering suspicions in post-Apartheid South Africa about the intentions and motivations of the West, these beliefs have led to conspiracy theories that question Western medicine (Nattrass 2012: 120–121). One of the most prevalent of these theories, which we include in our research, argues that birth control and condoms were created to control the Black population and should not be used.

United States

The last country we cover – the United States – is the country with the largest literature on conspiracy theories. Many (if not most) events in the country's history have triggered conspiracy theories. In addition to the international pandemic conspiracies and climate denialism, we focus on three contemporary American conspiracy theories in this Element. (1) The US government was involved in the attacks of 9/11, (2) former president Obama is lying about his birthplace, and (3) Joe Biden did not legitimately win the 2020 elections.

A relatively widespread conspiracy up to this day, the so-called Truther conspiracy, affirms that the Bush administration orchestrated the 9/11 attacks either alone or with the help of Al-Qaida to have a pretext to invade Afghanistan and then Iraq (Wood et al. 2012). According to the conspiracy theory, people within the government, including President Bush, planned and executed the 9/11 attacks with the help of Al-Qaida. The conspiracy theory also implies that Bush and his administration had sinister motives; they used the terrorist attack as a pretext to invade Iraq and gain control of the country's oil reserves (Bruder et al. 2013). The conspiracy started with anti-Bush protesters holding up signs "Bush knows" and then gained prominence when Democratic Congresswoman Cynthia McKinney asked for an official investigation to determine how much the Bush administration knew about the attacks beforehand. This more left-wing conspiracy has followers up to this day (see Byler and Woodsome 2021; Stockemer 2023).

Another theory, the so-called Birther conspiracy, follows an old playbook which politicians have used to denigrate a political rival by tagging them as non-American born. Most notably, this playbook was used against President Obama. According to birthers, the former US president was not born in the United States, but with the help of influential people in the government, he was able hide his real identity (Cheney 2016). According to the theory, Barack Obama is a Muslim born in Kenya. This theory began to spread from Illinois to the rest of the country, when Obama ran for president in 2008. Many Republicans, including Sarah Palin and Newt Gingrich, and most notably Donald Trump, supported the theory and have actively propagated it until today (Pasek et al. 2015).[7]

---

[7] In the 2024 Republican primaries, Donald Trump used the same playbook to attach Nikki Haley by spreading the lie that Haley is not American and instead born in India.

The third conspiracy theory we have decided to include is part of the canon of QAnon conspiracies. QAnon believers conceive of Donald Trump almost in a religious aspect, seeing him a "savior" against shadowy evildoers. Driven by this core belief that Donald Trump is a (near) religious figure, QAnon has exploded into a wide-reaching online and in-person community that interprets political events through their core conspiratorial lens. This includes the incorporation of new conspiracies in their belief system, most notably the "Big Lie" (Jacobson 2023). The Big Lie basically states that there was widespread elections fraud in the 2020 Presidential Elections and that Donald Trump was the legitimate winner (even though this affirmation has been strongly refuted by all available evidence). Baselessly, Donald Trump started to spread this lie before and even more strongly after the elections (Ntontis et al. 2024). The Big Lie is probably the most cited recent conspiracy theory in policy cycles up to this day (i.e., in 2024) (Arceneaux and Truex 2023).

3 How Widespread Are Conspiratorial Beliefs?

3.1 Existing literature

We know from previous research that conspiracy theories have spread across all continents and find their followers in every corner of the world (Hornsey et al. 2023; Stockemer and Bordeleau 2024). For example, in the United States, the literature reports that from one-fourth to one-third of the population believes in mainstream conspiracies including anti-COVID-19 ones (Uscinski et al. 2020). The literature reports similar numbers for other highly industrialized countries such as the United Kingdom and Canada (Freeman et al. 2022). In non-Western contexts, more mainstream conspiracy theories might see even greater support. The prime example is South Africa, where HIV/AIDS conspiracies have likely spread to among half of the population (Fassin 2007). More radical conspiracy theories may find fewer followers but can potentially still attract millions of believers. For instance, MacMillen and Rush (2022) argue that 20 percent or more Americans believe in part or fully in more obscure conspiracies such as QAnon. In other contexts, such as Germany, the most radical conspiracy theories, including the belief that the Jews were responsible for the start of World War II, might still attract up to 10 percent of the population (Haupt 1991).

Even though conspiracy theories exist in every corner of the world, the literature has not taken a global approach. The few attempts at comparative research have focused exclusively on Western countries (Bordeleau 2023; Walter and Drochon 2022). As of winter 2024, we have little knowledge on how strongly the same global conspiracies have spread across various contexts. Are there differences, for instance, in how strongly citizens believe in COVID-19 or climate change conspiracy theories between countries? What is more prevalent across the different contexts, country-specific conspiracy theories or more global ones? And lastly, can we say that citizens in one country are more likely to believe in conspiracy theories than citizens in another country?

We try to answer these questions in the pages to come. For each of the eight countries, we first present descriptive statistics on how many citizens believe in some international conspiracy theories and, if available, several country-specific ones. Finally, we try to decipher commonalities and differences between our six cases.

3.2 Conspiracy Beliefs across Our Eight Country Cases

3.2.1 Australia

Australia sees a relatively high level of conspiratorial beliefs. The theory which receives the highest backing is the one which argues that secret powers like the CIA or billionaire families control the world. In the Australian case, more than 30 percent of the surveyed state that this theory is either definitely or probably true (see Figure 1). Another nearly 30 percent are uncertain about its truth. If we look at the offspring of QAnon, which states that "pedophilic Satan-worshiping elites are trying to control our media and politics," our results indicate relatively strong support patterns (despite the radical nature of this theory), as well. In fact, roughly 22 percent of the surveyed either fully or likely concur with this theory. If we add the uncertain category to the equation, then we even have more than half of Australians who are either uncertain about or believe in this theory. The "home-made" conspiracy, which claims that the Chinese government had something to do with the disappearance of Prime Minister Harold Holt, finds somewhat less support. Only 17 percent find credence in this theory. However, what is striking is the high percentage of people in the uncertain category: nearly 37 percent of our participants have chosen this category (see Figure 1).

If we now turn to beliefs in the three global conspiracy theories, our results indicate that roughly 20 percent of the polled find any of the theories to be either probably or definitely true (see Figure 1). The numbers are slightly above 20 percent for the COVID-19 theories and a little below 20 percent for the climate change conspiracy theory. What is again striking is the high percentage of citizens in the middle category: roughly 25 percent of the surveyed declare that they are uncertain whether any of the three global conspiracies are true.

3.2.2 Brazil

Despite being a polarized country between Lulistas (supporters of the current president Lula) and Bolsanaristas (supporters of the former president Bolsonaro),

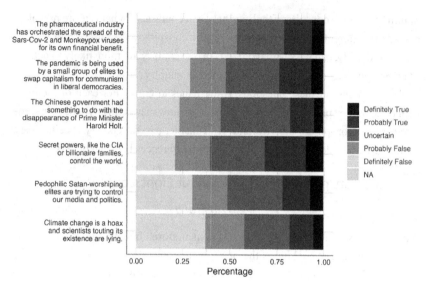

Figure 1 Beliefs in Conspiracy Theories in Australia

and despite some rampant supply of conspiracy theories, beliefs in these theories are quite moderate (see Figure 2) This applies particularly to the Brazilian version of the "Big Lie" or the affirmation that Lula stole the 2022 presidential election, and that Bolsonaro is the real winner (McKenna & O'Donnell 2024). Despite Bolsonaro and his supporters actively propagating this alternative reality in the aftermath of the 2022 election, this theory has gained very little traction in the Brazilian population. In fact, only around 10 percent of our sample think that this affirmation is either probably or definitely true.

The cultural Marxist version of the COVID-19 conspiracy theory has also gained relatively little traction in the Brazilian population. Notwithstanding Bolsonaro's emphasis on Cultural Marxism as a threat to the conservative Brazilian character, and him personally linking the cultural Marxist affirmation to the pandemic, only around 15 percent of our pool of respondents find the affirmation that elites use the pandemic to swap communism for capitalism credible. Another 15 percent are uncertain about this statement, and 70 percent refute it. Interestingly, the COVID-19 conspiracy that links the pandemic to the US's economic figureheads Bill Gates and George Soros has gained more traction. Only around 50 percent of our sample refute this theory. Another 27 percent are uncertain about it and 23 percent are either fully or likely in agreement with this theory. We can potentially explain the higher popularity of this theory by the tradition of anti-imperialism, nurturing anti-American sentiment and scapegoating the figureheads of American economic imperialism for

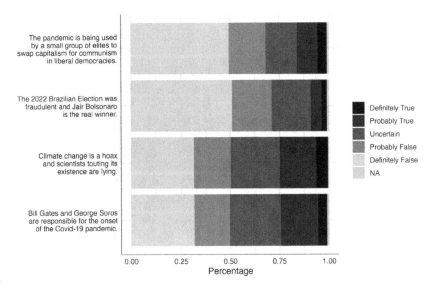

Figure 2 Beliefs in Conspiracy Theories in Brazil

domestic problems (Salles et al. 2023). We have similar approval numbers for the final conspiracy theory, which states that climate change is a hoax and scientists touting its existence are lying. Again, the number of followers for this theory stands at roughly 25 percent, if we combine the definitely true and probably true categories.

3.2.3 Canada

In Canada, there is quite some variation in beliefs in various conspiracy theories (see Figure 3). The conspiracy theories with the strongest support are the two right-wing political conspiracies: (1) Liberal media are paid actors working for Justin Trudeau, and (2) Liberals and environmental actors are working together to destroy Alberta's oil sands. Both conspiracies see the endorsement of more than one in four survey respondents. In addition, the first of these conspiracies also has a large portion of respondents being uncertain (37 percent). This implies that less than 40 percent of the survey participants fully or somewhat disagree with this theory. For the second right-wing conspiracy theory, our results illustrate that just over 50 percent of the sample disagree with this theory.

For the left-wing conspiracy theory in our sample (i.e., Pierre Poilievre is a Russian agent) we find less support. In fact, less than 14 percent of the survey respondents considered this theory probably true or definitely true. However, what is striking here, as well, is that over one-fourth of the surveyed are unsure about this statement. When it comes to the global conspiracy theories, we find

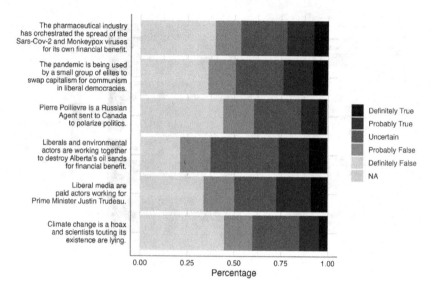

Figure 3 Beliefs in Conspiracy Theories in Canada

stronger support for the COVID-19 conspiracy theories than for the climate change one. Upward of 20 percent of the respondents agree that the pharmaceutical industry orchestrated the spread of the Sars-Cov-2 and Monkeypox viruses for its own financial benefit and that the pandemic is being used by a small group of elites to swap capitalism for communism in liberal democracies. In contrast, only 15 percent voice their support for the statement that climate change is a hoax. For all three theories, the percentage of the surveyed who indicate that they are unsure stands at exactly 25 percent for the three theories.

3.2.4 Germany

In Germany, we see a more nuanced picture. As expected, beliefs in the two radical conspiracy theories (i.e., Hitler did not die in 1945 but lived into his old age, and the Jews are responsible for World War II) receive comparatively little support (see Figure 4). Approximately 8 and 6 percent, respectively, find these theories to be probably or definitely true. While these support patterns are certainly low, they nevertheless translate into potentially millions of Germans believing in one, the other, or both theories. For the German version of QAnon, support is also low. Only roughly 10 percent of the surveyed believe the statement that past NATO operations in Germany were an operation by President Trump to liberate Germany from Chancellor Angela Merkel (see Figure 4). This also implies that QAnon has fewer followers in Germany than it has in Australia or the United States.

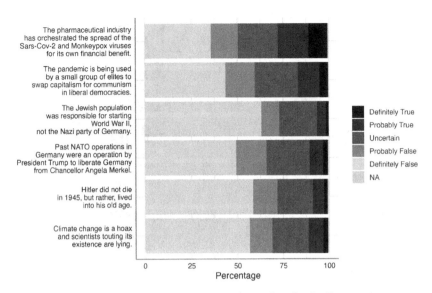

Figure 4 Beliefs in various conspiracy theories in Germany

When it comes to the global conspiracy theories, support for any of these theories is somewhat lower in Germany than it is in Australia and Canada. Support is also more fluctuating between the three theories. For example, a mere 11 percent of respondents agree with the statement that climate change is non-existent. For the two COVID-19 conspiracy theories, we see some differences in support. Roughly 16 percent of participants believe in the cultural Marxist COVID-19 conspiracy theory, whereas 27 percent are certain or see a high probability that the pharmaceutical industry orchestrated the COVID-19 pandemic for their own financial benefit. Especially for this latter theory this is a strong support pattern.

3.2.5 Lebanon

Lebanon presents a novel case. As expected, the two homegrown conspiracies regarding the Beirut explosion and the assassination of Rafic Hariri have gained relatively widespread support. Over 35 percent agree that the Beirut explosion was not an accident and 20 percent support the idea that the explosion and the assassination of Hariri are related (see Figure 5). The unknown nature of the Beirut explosion and the uncertain international environment render the idea of an "attack" or "plot" likely for many. Moreover, over 35 percent of respondents are uncertain of whether to think of the event as an accident or not.

In contrast, only 20 percent find it plausible that the two major catastrophes in Beirut (i.e., the assassination of Rafic Hariri and the Beirut explosion) are

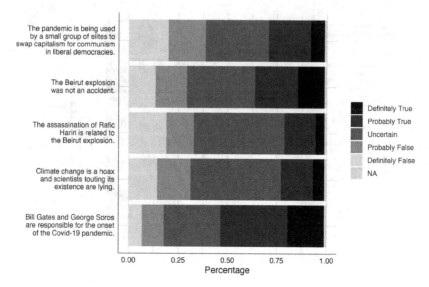

Figure 5 Beliefs in various conspiracy theories in Lebanon

related. Given the considerable time difference between the two events (i.e., fifteen years) the linkage between the two events just does not seem that probable. Nevertheless, and despite this implausibility, one in four respondents supports the idea that the two events are connected. When it comes to the two COVID-19 conspiracy theories, we find interesting patterns. There is particularly strong support for the anti-imperialist anti-Western theory: "Bill Gates and George Soros are responsible for the onset of the Covid-19 pandemic." Indeed, over 50 percent of respondents either probably or completely agree with this statement. In contrast, less than 18 percent consider this thesis definitely or probably false (see Figure 5).

Hence, this pandemic conspiracy theory is the perfect example of how large portions of the population can engage in blame attribution for a transboundary crisis. It is also interesting that the other COVID-19 conspiracy, the cultural Marxist one, only triggers support from less than 30 percent of the participants. Therefore, the example of these two pandemic-related conspiracies shows how conspiracies are an ideal tool to target an individual or group against whom the population already has some prejudices or negative predispositions. If we look at the last conspiracy theory on climate change, we again find that support for this theory is line with the patterns in other countries. Roughly 20 percent of the Lebanese respondents denied the existence of climate change with again a large section of the population being in the middle category.

3.2.6 Morocco

Looking at beliefs in conspiracy theories in Morocco, we find a noteworthy pattern (see Figure 6). For one, there is quite some variation between the three COVID-19 conspiracy theories, with the big pharma one triggering the most support and the Bill Gates and Soros one triggering the least support. In fact, more than one-third of our sample fully or probably agrees with the statement that big pharma orchestrated the SARS-Cov-2 and Monkeypox viruses for their own financial benefits. This number drops by roughly 10 points for the Bill Gates and George Soros one. Support for the cultural Marxist conspiracy lies in between the two other ones COVID-19 ones. Backing for the last conspiracy we asked – whether climate change is a hoax, and scientists are lying about its existence – is surprisingly very low. Only slightly above 10 percent of the people surveyed find this statement true or probably true.

Interestingly, and this corroborates the findings from Lebanon, even if the pattern is not as pronounced, we find that there is a high percentage of our sample who chooses the middle or uncertain category for all four conspiracy theories. This pattern is particularly pronounced for the cultural Marxist COVID-19 conspiracy theory and the climate change one. High levels of distrust with authorities and lack of credible information might explain why a plurality of respondents either do not want to take sides or cannot take sides. The high percentage of respondents in the uncertain camp also implies that for four of the five theories – the exception is the Bill Gates and George Soros

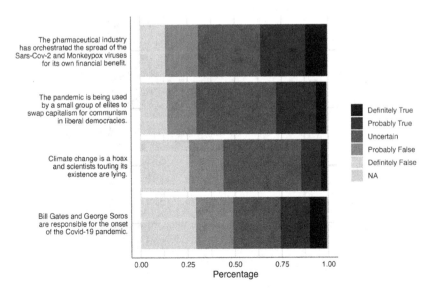

Figure 6 Beliefs in Conspiracy Theories in Morocco

conspiracy theory – a majority of our sample does not refute any of the four conspiracy theories. Rather, most of the surveyed are in the uncertain category.

3.2.7 South Africa

South Africa is another very interesting case, especially when it comes to belief patterns for country-specific conspiracy theories. We find considerable variation in the popularity of the three medical conspiracy theories. By far, the dominant theory is the one that states that the government and scientists have a cure for AIDS but are hiding its existence (see Figure 7). Indeed, more than 40 percent of respondents indicate their support for this theory and another 20 percent state that they are unsure. Potentially, belief in this conspiracy theory is spurred by some frustration that there is no real cure for Aids. Even more so, it might also stem from the long-lasting suspicion of Western science. The more radical HIV/ AIDS conspiracy theory – AIDS was created by white people to kill Black people – still finds support from more than 22 percent of the surveyed. These high support patterns could be a manifestation of how deeply engrained suspicion and hatred toward the white population is among parts of the Black population. Finally, less than 17 percent of the surveyed agree with the statement that birth control and condoms were created to control the Black population and should not be used.

Pertaining to the COVID-19 conspiracies, we find suspicion toward the virus to be high. Roughly 33 percent of the polled believe in the two COVID-19

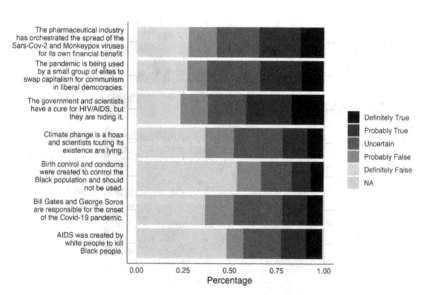

Figure 7 Beliefs in Conspiracy Theories in South Africa

conspiracies (the cultural Marxist one and the one that attributes the blame for the pandemic to the pharmaceutical industry). Given the clear suspicion toward science, these relatively high numbers are expected. For the two COVID-19 conspiracies, we also find upward of 25 percent in the uncertain category, which renders the percentage of the polled who refute both conspiracy theories to stand at roughly 40 percent. Interestingly, there is some less support for the third COVID-19 conspiracy theory which links the pandemic's outbreak to figure-heads of US's economic domination, namely Bill Gates and George Soros. Finally, support for the climate change conspiracy theory is somewhat lower and in line with support patterns in other countries. Just around one in five respondents from South Africa do not believe in climate change (see Figure 7).

3.2.8 United States

Across the four Western countries we include in our analyses, the United States is the country with the highest support for conspiracy theories. It is also the country where we find the least variation in belief patterns for any conspiracy theory. Support for the six theories we ask fluctuates between 23 and 33 percent (see Figure 8). The theory that triggers the least support – but still the highest support across the six countries – is the climate change denial conspiracy theory. In this case, 23 percent of the surveyed indicate that they agree with the idea that climate change is not real. Support for all remaining conspiracy theories is above 25 percent (see Figure 8). While we probably expect such high levels of

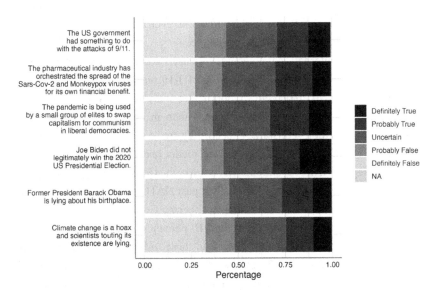

Figure 8 Beliefs in Conspiracy Theories in the United States

support for the COVID-19 conspiracies, we do not necessarily expect this for the more radical theories such as those thematizing the US government's involvement in the events surrounding 9/11.

We further find that 28 percent of the answers agree with the 9/11 conspiracy theory. Having nearly 30 percent of the population considering their government's involvement in one of the worst catastrophes in the country's history is concerning. It is equally concerning that 32 percent believe that Joe Biden did not legitimately win the 2020 elections. The Big Lie conspiracy is also the conspiracy in our sample where the most people indicate "definitely true." Given these numbers, it comes to no surprise that another 26 percent of those surveyed agree with the conspiracy theory according to which Barack Obama was not born in the United States.

3.3 Discussion

In the eight countries we study, conspiracy theories are mainstream. Indeed, in any of the eight countries, there is at least one conspiracy which triggers the support of more than one in four respondents. Of the global conspiracy theories, we find that, with some exception for Brazil, those related to COVID-19 are more popular than the climate change one. In early 2023, when we conducted the survey, there was still widespread suspicion regarding the existence and origin of the Sars-Cov-2 virus. In most countries, around 30 percent share this suspicion and attribute blame to some nebulous elites and/or the pharmaceutical complex (see Figure 9). The high levels of belief in some countries (e.g., Australia or Canada) in the cultural Marxist version also show the potential to combine one conspiracy theory with another one even if the two are completely unrelated, and potentially mutually exclusive.

For the second international conspiracy theory, denial of climate change, we find that it is less pronounced than the COVID-19 ones but depending on the context still upward of 20 percent support it. Our study also illustrates that some conspiracies spread more in some contexts than in others. For example, in Australia, the QAnon conspiracy according to which pedophilic Satan-worshiping elites are trying to control the media and politics resonates with more than 20 percent of respondents. In contrast, the German version of QAnon, which is less radical and "only" affirms that past NATO operations in Germany were an operation by President Trump to liberate Germany from Chancellor Angela Merkel, finds support in less than 10 percent of the surveyed. For the more country-specific conspiracies, we find these to be particularly strong in South Africa and Lebanon, where upward 40 percent believe at least in one of them. Even if the numbers do not reach 40 percent, domestic conspiracies also

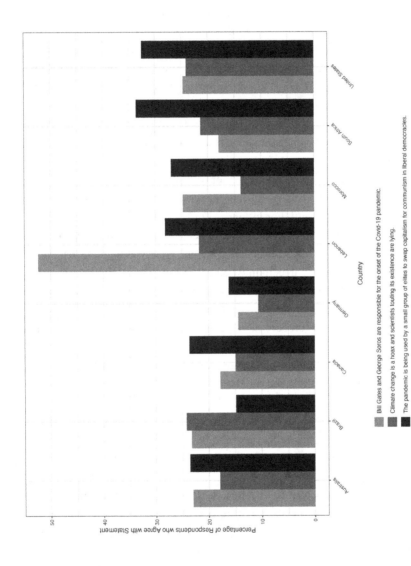

Figure 9 Belief in three specific conspiracy theories across eight countries

resonate in the United States. In fact, the Big Lie, which one-third of the population supports, is among the most popular conspiracies we have studied in that country.

What we also find striking is that a large portion of respondents situate themselves in the middle or uncertain category (see Figure 10). This percentage is higher for the COVID-19 conspiracy theories compared to the climate change one. For example, throughout the sample, nearly 30 percent place themselves in the uncertain category for the two COVID-19 conspiracy theories. For Lebanon this number spikes to over 50 percent for the Bill Gates and George Soros COVID-19 conspiracy theory. For the climate change is a hoax conspiracy theory, the percentage of respondents in the uncertain category still fluctuates around 20 percent, with a peak in the United States where roughly 25 percent of the surveyed claim to be uncertain about the existence of climate change.

The high percentage of individuals in the uncertain category is not restricted to global or international conspiracy theories. For some country-specific conspiracy theories, the percentage of individuals in the uncertain category also reaches more than one third. For instance, 37 percent of respondents in Canada are uncertain whether Liberals and environmental actors are working together to destroy Alberta's oil sands for financial benefit. Nearly as high, 35 percent of Lebanese respondents are uncertain whether the Beirut explosion was an accident; this number even reaches 46 percent for the second conspiracy in Lebanon which establishes a connection between the assassination of Rafic Hariri and the Beirut explosion. For Morocco, more people are in the uncertain camp than either in the pro- or anti-conspiracy theory camp in three of the four theories we cover. Even some very radical conspiracy theories such as the two German ones concerning whether Hitler lived on after 1945 and that the Jewish population was responsible for starting World War II trigger 20 percent in the uncertain category. Future research should determine why so many people choose the middle category: Does this reflect genuine uncertainty, is the middle category a convenient option, or do they lack the political knowledge to position themselves on the Likert scales?

More generally, we want to end this section with a word of caution. The Likert scales we use to measure conspiracy theory beliefs only provide an approximation of the real number of believers in conspiracy theories. For one, these measures might be inflated due to acquiescence bias. Acquiescence bias refers to the potential of people to agree to questions, regardless of the questions' content (Clifford et al. 2019; Hill and Roberts 2023). Because we ask respondents in our surveys if they agree with specific conspiracy theories (rather than disagree), we might predispose them to answer in the affirmative. In contrast, there is also the potential of social desirability bias. Social desirability

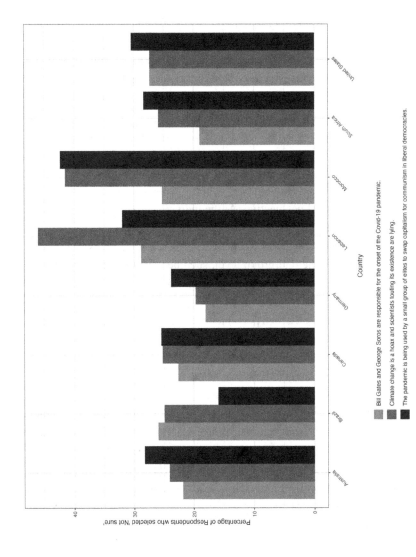

Figure 10 Percentage of respondents in the uncertain category for international conspiracy theories

bias refers to citizens' potential to give politically correct answers in surveys for sensitive topics rather than exposing their true beliefs (Lantian et al. 2018; Smallpage et al. 2023). Exposing one's own belief in a conspiracy theory is certainly a sensitive topic, and individuals might opt for the politically correct option when asked about a conspiracy theory in surveys to look good or mainstream, rather than extreme. Unfortunately, we cannot detect the level of both acquiescence bias and social desirability bias. One bias might be stronger than the other; it might also be that these two countervailing tendencies balance each other out. However, what we can say is that some respondents who situate themselves in the uncertain category might find answering the middle category an easy way out, which allows them to give a half-way socially correct answer, while not (fully) denying their true beliefs.

Despite these caveats, we find high levels of support for conspiracy theories concerning. Support of 20, 30, or more percent for specific conspiracy illustrates that in each country there are millions of people who believe in these unfounded claims. These high support patterns are detrimental both from an individual and a societal perspective. At the individual level, there is evidence that believing in conspiracy theories is linked to lesser care of one's own health, lower subjective well-being, and weakened social relationships (van Prooijen et al. 2022). More on the intergroup level, such beliefs also increase negative stereotyping and might inspire individuals to use violence (Douglas et al. 2015).[8]

On a more societal level, a high percentage of citizens believing in conspiracy theories can have detrimental consequences. If a large portion of citizens cannot distinguish fiction from reality and live in alternate conspiratorial universes, then democracy is in danger. It is in danger because the same forces that propagate conspiracy theories frequently also reject liberal democracy and the rule of law (Hidalgo 2022; Moore 2018). Well-known actors in the conspiracy theory camp are Donald Trump and Jair Bolsonaro. Both former presidents have baselessly propagated their version of the Big Lie, thus delegitimizing democracy and jeopardizing the existence of free and fair elections. Other conspiracy theories such as the COVID-19 conspiracies, or the domestic medically related conspiracies in South Africa question science and medicine, and potentially hurt efforts to contain a virus or pandemic.

---

[8] Even if the belief in conspiracy theories is only one of many factors that can incite individuals to use violence (see also Uscinski et al. 2022), it is still concerning that belief in misinformation and conspiracy theories can render the use of violence legitimate for some people.

4 Who Believes in Conspiracy Theories?

4.1 Explaining Conspiracy Beliefs

Given the prevalence of conspiracy theories in our eight cases, it is of the utmost importance to determine what types of characteristics are conducive to the spread of conspiracy beliefs. In the pages to come, we distinguish between sociopolitical, psychological, and demographic correlates of conspiracy beliefs. We also discuss whether belief in one conspiracy theory is likely to result in belief in others, and whether such systematic structure in the individual-level determinants of conspiracy theory beliefs is the same regardless of space.

4.1.1 Sociopolitical Factors

Sociopolitical factors are an important type of explanatory variables for explaining conspiracy beliefs. We include in our analyses seven of the most studied sociopolitical factors from the conspiracy theory literature; these include education, economic status, political ideology, political interest, populist attitudes, satisfaction with democracy, and religiosity.

For education, we believe that more educated individuals should be less likely to believe in conspiracy theories. This follows many previous studies which demonstrate a negative relationship between education levels and conspiracy beliefs. According to van Prooijen (2017), for example, more educated citizens should have higher analytical cognitive capacities, which, in turn, should diminish the search for simple solutions. More educated people should also be more likely to see through the speculative/faulty nature of conspiracy theories (Georgiou et al. 2019; Imhoff et al. 2022).

For the second factor, economic status, we expect a similar relationship as for education: individuals with higher economic status should be less likely to believe in conspiracy theories (Mao et al. 2020). For one, wealthier individuals normally live in a more well-kept environment, they have ample opportunities both socially and professionally, and they may feel in control of their lives (Kraus et al. 2012). In contrast, less well-off citizens frequently struggle to make ends meet and live in harsher environments both personally and professionally (Li et al. 2018). Such environments are less conducive to feeling safe and confident. Particularly, a feeling of lack of self-control might render low-income individuals more likely to turn to conspiracy theories than higher income earners.

The next indicator is political ideology. In Western countries, particularly, most conspiracy theories are ideological tainted. In the words of Thórisdóttir et al. (2020), conspiracy theories are a product of extremism. Imhoff et al.

(2022) nuance these findings: according to the authors, conspiratorial beliefs are strongest on the left and right. Yet, their findings provide some room for debate. Indeed, they find that the relationship between ideology and conspiracy beliefs is more complex than expected, with individuals in the center of the political orientation scale also scoring high on conspiracy belief scales. They demonstrate that we can explain some of these differences by the political context in which individuals live, highlighting for instance the role of the political party in power or the salience of ideology in a given context. Building on Imhoff et al. (2022) we find it intriguing to test whether the effects of political ideology are really stronger on the fringes, or whether there is contextual variation.

When it comes to political interest, we see two possible outcomes. On the one hand, politically interested citizens should be more likely to refrain from believing in conspiracy theories. Knowledge of the complexity of the political system and the implausibility of conspiracy theories should act as a bulwark against these beliefs (Räikkä 2009). On the other hand, we know that conspiracy theories spread on the extremes of the ideological spectrum, and citizens with such extreme political attitudes are often very politically interested, even if it is only to consume and spread radical messages such as conspiracy theories (Kim 2022).

For the fifth factor – populist attitudes – we expect a strong and positive relationship with conspiracy beliefs (Erisen et al. 2021). Populism and conspiracy theories are related ideologically since they are both supportive of the rejection and suspicion of elites (Christner 2022). Both populism and conspiracy theories also try to find a scapegoat for social or political events, and both have a Manichean view of the world that divides society into the virtuous and the evil (Galais and Rico 2021). Frequently, conspiracy theories are also a means by populists to attack elites. Accordingly, we expect populist attitudes and conspiracy beliefs to be strongly related.

Next, we believe that political dissatisfaction is likely an important precondition for individuals to believe in conspiracy theories. Conspiracy theories assume the existence of sinister forces or elites who try to harm the public or a segment of the population (Schlipphak et al. 2022). People who have strong feelings of dissatisfaction against the government (or any other elite) are likely to believe a narrative that blames these already disliked group (Karić and Međedović 2021), which, in turn, should make them more susceptible to adhere to conspiracy beliefs targeting these elites.

Finally, we expect to see a positive relationship between religiosity and conspiracy theories. Most importantly, the underlying mechanisms that make people believe in religion and conspiracy theories are similar. Both fulfill similar psychological needs (i.e., they provide meaning and belonging), provide answers to unanswerable questions, and allow followers to explain the world around them in simple terms (Frenken et al. 2023). Highlighting the similarity between the two concepts, Franks et al. (2013) ascribe to conspiracy theories quasi-religious qualities. This implies that individuals drawn to religion might also have a higher tendency to be drawn to conspiracy theories. This applies even more so considering that conspiracy theories play a crucial role in religious fundamentalism (Dyrendal 2020).

4.1.2 Psychological Factors

We add two psychological factors to our analysis, both of which have been extensively linked to conspiracy beliefs: self-esteem and need for closure. In terms of individual's self-esteem, there are three possible mechanisms which could draw individuals toward conspiracy theories (Swami et al. 2014). First, people with low self-esteem are not as outgoing and lack integration into society. Believing in conspiracy theories, which in their view is knowledge that other people do not have, could help them overcome these feelings of being left behind (Cichocka et al. 2016). Second, and relatedly, the belief in conspiracy theories gives them the illusion that they possess the answer to an event that other individuals do not have. This, in turn, could give them a feeling of being more knowledgeable and intelligent than others are (Lantian et al. 2017). Third, the psychological literature has established that people with low self-esteem tend to see the world more negatively (Baumeister et al. 2005; Kőszegi et al. 2022). By definition conspiracy theories are negative and assume the existence of sinister forces who want to ruin the world. As such, conspiracy theories should attract individuals with lower self-esteem; as they allow them to "blame others for their problems" (Abalakina-Paap et al. 1999: 644).

For the second psychological factor, we expect to find a strong positive relationship between need for cognitive closure and conspiracy theory endorsement (Leman and Cinnirella 2013; Marchlewska et al. 2018). Events that lend themselves to conspiracy theories are frequently events that make people feel uneasy. These include catastrophes, terror attacks, or pandemics to name but a few. These events also open the way for speculation, especially if the official answer is not clear or contested by elites (Umam et al. 2018). Conspiracy theories can therefore provide a simple answer to a complex scenario – an answer that also clearly delineates who are the good people and who are the bad people. Such a black-and-white answer might be attractive for individuals who have higher levels of need for cognitive closure.

4.1.3 Demographics and Personal Characteristics

For the last type of variables – demographic factors – we include gender, age, and place of residence (urban/rural). When it comes to gender, there is some evidence indicating that men have an increased tendency to believe in conspiracy theories (Cassese et al. 2020; Popoli and Longus 2021). According to recent psychological research (see Farhart et al. 2022; Šrol et al. 2021), men score higher in learned helplessness, a condition of feeling powerless, which might stem from a lack of success or traumatic events. This, in turn, may explain their increased tendency to believe in conspiracy theories.

The second demographic factor we test for is age. Even if not all studies either include age in their analyses or discuss the effects of age in the body of their manuscript (see Bordeleau and Stockemer 2024b), those that do generally find that younger adults are more attuned to believing in conspiracy theories than older adults (Freeman et al. 2022; Uscinski et al. 2020). Youth look for something new, do not have set political ideologies, and often feel attracted to extremes (Pollock et al. 2015). Together, these factors could explain their higher tendency to believe in conspiracy theories.

Finally, we add place of residence (urban/rural) into our models. We expect citizens who live in the countryside to be more likely to be attracted to conspiracy theories (Al-Wutayd et al. 2021). Countryside residents are often more right-wing, and they might form isolated communities, which might not be well connected to information sources. Rural dwellers might also be more critical toward globalization, pluralism, and international elites because of their geographic situation (Duncan 2001). All these factors could foster individuals' increased likelihoods to adhere to conspiracy theories.

We rely on these three types of indicators – sociopolitical, psychological, and demographic – to understand the constituents of conspiracy theory beliefs and the moderating influence country context might have. We are particularly curious to determine if the same or different factors explain beliefs in conspiracy theories across different national contexts.

4.1.4 Operationalization of Independent Factors

This section discusses how we operationalize the different independent factors presented in the first parts of this section. The complete list of scales and items used to operationalize our variables is available in the supplementary material (see Supplementary Table 1).

In terms of demographic variables, we measure age on a continuous scale beginning at eighteen and gender using a dichotomous indicator where 0 = female and 1 = male. We also capture the place of residence using a 5-point measure, where 1 = a big city; 2 = a suburb or outskirt of a big city; 3 = a town or small city; 4 = a village; and 5 = the countryside.

In terms of the sociopolitical factors, we rely on a 5-point self-declared education-level scale, where 1 = no formal education; 2 = elementary education; 3 = secondary education; 4 = college/university education; and 5 = postgraduate education. We capture socioeconomic status using a trichotomous self-declared item – "Financially-speaking, in your country, would you say you are a part of the lower-class, middle-class, or the upper-class?" – with answers ranging from 1 = lower class; 2 = middle class; and 3 = upper class. For political ideology, we rely on the following commonly used item: "In politics people sometimes talk of left and right. Where would you place yourself on a scale from 0 to 10 where 0 means the left and 10 means the right?" Political interest is also captured on an 11-point item – "How interested are you in politics?" – with 0 = not at all interested to 11 = very interested. For populist attitudes, we use the 8-item scale developed by Akkerman et al. (2014) and measure it on 5-point Likert scales (1 = low populist attitudes; 5 = high populist attitudes; see supplementary material for full-scale item wording). We rely on the following item to measure respondent's satisfaction with democracy in their country: "How satisfied are you with the way democracy works in [country]?" Answers have an 11-point scale ranging from 0 = not satisfied at all; to 10 = very satisfied. Lastly, we measure religiosity via a dichotomous item, where 0 = not religious; and 1 = religious.

For the psychological factors, we rely primarily on existing scales widely used in psychological research. In more detail, we measure self-esteem using the 10-item Rosenberg scale (Rosenberg 1965) and index mean scores to form a unique self-esteem value ranging from 0 = low self-esteem; to 3 = high self-esteem. Lastly, we gauge need for cognitive closure using the 15-item scale indexed into a single score from 1 = low need for closure; to 5 = high need for closure (Roets and Van Hiel 2011).

4.2 Is There a Systematic Structure in the Individual Determinants of Conspiracy Beliefs ?

In addition to establishing the factors that explain beliefs in conspiracy theories and whether these differ across contexts, we are interested in identifying whether the profile of a conspiracy theory believer is different for some conspiracy theories compared to others. In other words, we are interested in whether the correlates of conspiracy theory beliefs are the same for all conspiracy theories we study or only for specific ones. The more we find homogeneity in belief patterns across various conspiracy theories, the more we can talk of what is referred to in the literature as a systematic structure in the individual-level determinants of conspiracy theory beliefs (or conspiracy thinking). The idea of such a systematic structure was first pronounced by Goertzel (1994). He argues that people who believe in one conspiracy theory generally believe in other ones, as well, cascading through a hermetic network of conspiratorial theories. In the words of Douglas et al. (2019: 7), individuals bouncing from one conspiracy theory to the next constitute a "monological belief system" where belief in one theory will lead to belief in several others.

Miller et al. ((2016) further suggest that individuals who believe in conspiracy theories tend to engage in motivated reasoning (Douglas et al. 2019; Miller et al. 2016) which involves seeking out "information that confirms what they already believe" (Min 2021: 416). This results in individuals interpreting "new information in such a way as to not disturb their previously held worldviews" (Douglas et al. 2019: 12). A relevant example is Gemenis' (2021) study of COVID-19 skeptics in Greece, where he finds that belief in COVID-19 conspiracy theories are correlated with belief in other unrelated conspiracy theories tackling the Greek financial crisis or the infamous Chemtrails theory.[9]

In this study, it is our goal to determine the boundary conditions of the thesis of a systematic structure in the individual-level determinants of conspiracy theory beliefs. Are believers of conspiracy theories similar regardless of the type of conspiracy theory? Or is this conspiratorial "contagion" restricted to similar conspiracy theories such as politically motivated right-wing conspiracies?

4.3 Results

Using data from the Comparative Conspiracy Research Survey (see section 1; Bordeleau et al. 2023), we present ordinary least square regression models with determinants of conspiracy beliefs per country. We are particularly interested in determining if there is a prototypical conspiracy believer, or, in other words, whether the same factors explain conspiracy beliefs across context and different types of conspiracy theories. We present the results by country and provide a general discussion afterward.

---

[9] The Chemtrails conspiracy theory assumes that that governments or any other third-party use aircrafts to spray toxic chemicals into the atmosphere aiming to sterilize the population, decrease life expectancy, control the minds of citizens, or influence the weather patterns (Bantimaroudis 2016; Cairns 2016).

4.3.1 Australia

The determinants of the typical conspiracy believer in Australia are analogous across the six theories we cover. An Australian conspiracy theory believer shares six main characteristics. He/she is rather young, to the right of the ideological spectrum, displays populist attitudes, is dissatisfied with democracy, rather religious, and has low self-esteem (see Table 2)

Interestingly, these same six predictors of conspiracy theory beliefs are statistically significant in all six models, regardless of whether we look at a more global conspiracy theories (e.g., the pandemic is being used by a small group of elites to swap capitalism for communism in liberal democracies) or more Australia-specific conspiracies (e.g., the Chinese government had something to do with the disappearance of Prime Minister Harold Holt). The magnitude of the regression coefficients for these six variables is also quite similar across the six conspiracy theories we cover. This implies that, in Australia, the same factors explain beliefs in different conspiracy theories. Overall, this suggests the presence of a systematic structure in the individual-level determinants of conspiracy theory beliefs, at least for Australia.

There is also a very clear-cut distinction between statistically significant and statistically nonsignificant variables. Except for the tendency of rural residents to have a higher likelihood to believe in climate change denial, none of the other explanatory variables show any statistically significant relationships in any of the models.

4.3.2 Brazil

For Brazil our regression analysis (see Table 3) reveals that most of the same variables as in Australia remain relevant; these are a rightist ideology, populist attitudes, religiosity, and a lack of self-esteem. What changes is that age loses its statistical significance. This might be due to the younger population in this Latin American continent. Compared to the Australian case, the Brazilian case also adds some nuance. For example, there is a (small) positive effect between lower education and higher support for any of the four conspiracy theories. What also sticks out and this is remarkable is that we find support for the thesis of a systematic structure in the individual-level determinants of conspiracy theory beliefs. Despite the fact that the four conspiracy theories we cover have widely different topics (i.e., the pandemic, climate change, and the country's presidential election in 2022), we find that mainly the same factors explain beliefs in such theories; these factors are a right-wing ideology, populist attitudes, religious belief, and low self-esteem. Especially, the latter, a low self-esteem appears to have a strong influence. We find that a one-point increase in self-

Table 2 Determinants of Beliefs in Various Conspiracy Theories Australia

	Climate Change	Pandemic Communism	China and PM Holt	Pedophilic Elites	Big Pharma Pandemic	CIA and Billionaires
(Intercept)	1.346***	0.892*	1.507***	1.280**	1.530***	1.152**
	(0.366)	(0.398)	(0.349)	(0.393)	(0.387)	(0.407)
Age	−0.023***	−0.013***	−0.022***	−0.021***	−0.023***	−0.016***
	(0.003)	(0.003)	(0.003)	(0.003)	(0.003)	(0.003)
Gender	−0.074	−0.038	−0.014	0.011	0.126	0.074
	(0.078)	(0.085)	(0.075)	(0.084)	(0.083)	(0.087)
Education	0.007	−0.050	−0.015	−0.046	−0.058	−0.064
	(0.042)	(0.045)	(0.040)	(0.045)	(0.044)	(0.046)
Urban/Rural	−0.136**	−0.073	−0.070	−0.055	−0.096+	−0.012
	(0.047)	(0.051)	(0.045)	(0.050)	(0.049)	(0.052)
Economic Status	0.033	0.021	0.118	−0.004	−0.117	0.038
	(0.077)	(0.084)	(0.074)	(0.083)	(0.081)	(0.086)
Political Ideology	0.124***	0.154***	0.096***	0.118***	0.118***	0.098***
	(0.019)	(0.020)	(0.018)	(0.020)	(0.020)	(0.021)
Political Interest	0.010	0.006	0.002	0.014	0.020	0.024
	(0.014)	(0.016)	(0.014)	(0.015)	(0.015)	(0.016)
SWD	−0.050**	−0.049**	−0.055***	−0.054**	−0.042*	−0.081***

	(1)	(2)	(3)	(4)	(5)	(6)
Populist Attitudes	0.142*	0.211**	0.180**	0.223***	0.164*	0.344***
	(0.016)	(0.018)	(0.016)	(0.018)	(0.017)	(0.018)
Religiosity	0.342***	0.236**	0.295***	0.365***	0.254**	0.205*
	(0.060)	(0.065)	(0.058)	(0.065)	(0.064)	(0.067)
Need for Closure	0.110	0.136+	0.099	0.132+	0.177*	0.109
	(0.081)	(0.088)	(0.077)	(0.087)	(0.085)	(0.090)
Self-Esteem	−0.175**	−0.201**	−0.163*	−0.197**	−0.204**	−0.181*
	(0.075)	(0.081)	(0.071)	(0.080)	(0.079)	(0.083)
	(0.066)	(0.072)	(0.063)	(0.071)	(0.070)	(0.073)
N	798	795	797	798	798	798
R^2	0.266	0.186	0.245	0.216	0.225	0.180
Log Likelihood	−1167.20	−1228.31	−1129.38	−1224.50	−1210.50	−1251.65
RMSE	1.04	1.13	1.00	1.12	1.10	1.16

+ $p < 0.1$, * $p < 0.05$, ** $p < 0.01$, *** $p < 0.001$

Table 3 Determinants of Beliefs in Various Conspiracy Theories Brazil

	Climate Change	Pandemic Communism	Gates and Soros COVID	2022 Election Was Fraudulent
(Intercept)	1.408**	0.920+	1.302*	1.506**
	(0.517)	(0.509)	(0.531)	(0.458)
Age	0.001	0.004	−0.001	0.001
	(0.003)	(0.003)	(0.004)	(0.003)
Gender	−0.138	0.193*	−0.077	−0.062
	(0.092)	(0.091)	(0.095)	(0.082)
Education	−0.230**	−0.170*	−0.153+	−0.176*
	(0.086)	(0.085)	(0.088)	(0.076)
Urban/Rural	−0.077+	0.009	0.036	−0.063
	(0.046)	(0.045)	(0.047)	(0.040)
Economic Status	0.069	0.180*	0.188*	0.117
	(0.090)	(0.088)	(0.092)	(0.079)
Political Ideology	0.107***	0.097***	0.094***	0.052***
	(0.014)	(0.014)	(0.015)	(0.013)
Political Interest	−0.005	−0.005	−0.023	−0.009
	(0.017)	(0.017)	(0.018)	(0.015)
SWD	−0.036*	0.001	−0.012	−0.006

	(0.015)	(0.014)	(0.015)	(0.013)
Populist Attitudes	0.260***	0.057	0.274***	0.161**
	(0.070)	(0.068)	(0.072)	(0.061)
Religiosity	0.210*	0.139	0.184+	−0.043
	(0.106)	(0.104)	(0.109)	(0.094)
Need for Closure	−0.004	0.019	−0.059	−0.046
	(0.082)	(0.081)	(0.084)	(0.073)
Self-Esteem	−0.250**	−0.360***	−0.392***	−0.327***
	(0.086)	(0.084)	(0.088)	(0.076)
N	670	666	669	668
R^2	0.156	0.131	0.136	0.082
Log Likelihood	−1043.394	−1022.087	−1057.985	−955.672
RMSE	1.15	1.12	1.18	1.01

+ $p < 0.1$, * $p < 0.05$, ** $p < 0.01$, *** $p < 0.001$

esteem reduces someone's likelihood to believe in conspiracy theories by roughly .3 points. This implies that someone at the bottom of the self-esteem scales has a 1.2-point higher likelihood to believe in conspiracy theories, which is a substantive change on the 5-item Likert scale.

4.3.3 Canada

When it comes to the correlates of conspiracy theory beliefs, Canadian respondents are very similar to Australian respondents. The typical Canadian conspiracy believer is of young age, to the right of the political spectrum, dissatisfied with how democracy works in Canada, religious, and has low levels of self-esteem (see Table 4). In terms of strength, populist attitudes and low self-esteem also seem to have the strongest effect. For example, most models predict that populist attitudes can increase someone's predicted likelihood to believe in any of the six conspiracy theories by up to 2 points on the 5-point scale, which is quite large. While we find the general tendencies in the typical conspiracy believer to be similar to those in Australia and Brazil, we also find some modest variation. For instance, higher education seems to reduce someone's tendency to believe in some but not all conspiracies covered. In particular, people with high education seem to have a lower likelihood to believe in politically motivated conspiracies (e.g., Liberals and environmental actors are working together to destroy Alberta's oil sands for financial benefit). We also do not find support for the thesis that climate change denial is larger in the countryside, unlike in Australia.

There are also some surprising findings. Based on the regression results, it seems that people who classify themselves to the right are still more likely to believe the statement that Conservative Leader Pierre Poilievre is a Russian Agent, even if this is clearly a left-wing conspiracy theory conceived to discredit the right-wing leader Poilievre. There is even a second nuance in Canada concerning the Pierre Poilievre conspiracy. In fact, people who are more satisfied with democracy are more likely to believe in this conspiracy, whereas for the other five conspiracies, it is the less satisfied who have a higher chance to recur to these.

4.3.4 Germany

Results for Germany are also largely in line with those of Australia, Canada, and to a slightly lesser degree Brazil. The same six characteristics (i.e., a young age, a right-wing political ideology, populist attitudes, dissatisfaction with democracy, religiosity, and low self-esteem) that are relevant in Australia and Canada also bear explanatory influence in Western Europe's largest democracy (see

Table 4 Determinants of Beliefs in Various Conspiracy Theories Canada

	Climate Change	Pandemic Communism	Liberal Environment	Liberal Media	Big Pharma Pandemic	Poilievre Russia
(Intercept)	1.071**	0.743+	1.150**	0.626	1.471***	1.520***
	(0.390)	(0.424)	(0.392)	(0.419)	(0.406)	(0.398)
Age	−0.015***	−0.015***	−0.005+	−0.008**	−0.018***	−0.018***
	(0.003)	(0.003)	(0.003)	(0.003)	(0.003)	(0.003)
Gender	0.001	−0.036	−0.025	0.084	0.007	−0.006
	(0.076)	(0.083)	(0.077)	(0.082)	(0.080)	(0.078)
Education	−0.050	−0.091	−0.153*	−0.085	−0.159*	−0.162**
	(0.061)	(0.066)	(0.061)	(0.065)	(0.063)	(0.062)
Urban/Rural	−0.031	0.032	−0.007	0.025	0.028	−0.044
	(0.034)	(0.037)	(0.034)	(0.036)	(0.035)	(0.034)
Economic Status	−0.072	−0.047	−0.028	0.001	0.021	0.089
	(0.081)	(0.088)	(0.081)	(0.087)	(0.084)	(0.082)
Political Ideology	0.125***	0.142***	0.189***	0.177***	0.158***	0.090***
	(0.018)	(0.019)	(0.018)	(0.019)	(0.018)	(0.018)
Political Interest	0.020	0.021	0.007	0.023	0.006	−0.012
	(0.014)	(0.015)	(0.014)	(0.015)	(0.015)	(0.014)

Table 4 (cont.)

	Climate Change	Pandemic Communism	Liberal Environment	Liberal Media	Big Pharma Pandemic	Poilievre Russia
SWD	-0.055***	-0.083***	-0.087***	-0.127***	-0.089***	0.066***
	(0.015)	(0.016)	(0.015)	(0.016)	(0.015)	(0.015)
Populist Attitudes	0.374***	0.493***	0.485***	0.544***	0.444***	0.238***
	(0.057)	(0.062)	(0.058)	(0.062)	(0.060)	(0.058)
Religiosity	0.302***	0.282***	0.114	0.204*	0.300***	0.192*
	(0.078)	(0.085)	(0.079)	(0.084)	(0.082)	(0.080)
Need for Closure	-0.068	0.010	-0.105	-0.089	-0.073	-0.003
	(0.068)	(0.074)	(0.068)	(0.073)	(0.071)	(0.069)
Self-Esteem	-0.309***	-0.297***	-0.265***	-0.298***	-0.334***	-0.405***
	(0.066)	(0.072)	(0.067)	(0.071)	(0.069)	(0.067)
N	803	802	799	801	802	796
R^2	0.296	0.321	0.341	0.365	0.367	0.252
Log Likelihood	-1158.813	-1222.784	-1154.711	-1212.684	-1189.015	-1157.912
RMSE	1.02	1.11	1.03	1.10	1.07	1.04

+ p < 0.1, * p < 0.05, ** p < 0.01, *** p < 0.001

Table 5). Similarly to the previous countries, populist attitudes and lack of self-esteem appear to be strong factors, even if their predicted effect appears to fluctuate a bit between the models (i.e., between one and two points on the five points' conspiracy theory beliefs Likert scale). There is also some nuance in the Germany model, in that there is a seventh and, to a lesser degree, eight factor that stick out. In Germany, education seems to be a bulwark against conspiracy belief, with more highly educated individuals displaying a lower propensity to belief in such theories. The eighth factor is gender, with women being less likely to believe in four of the six theories. Interestingly, it is only the two most radical theories (i.e., the Jews are responsible for the onset of World War II, and Hitler did not die in 1945 but lived to old age) which do not trigger a gender difference in support. Another nuance is that religiosity also does not seem to influence beliefs in the theory that the pharmaceutical industry has orchestrated the spread of Sars-Cov-2 and Monkeypox viruses.

Germany is also interesting because it allows us to test whether the determinants of niche and radical theories differ from those of more mainstream and less radical theories. We find that this is not the case. Aside from some slight differences when it comes to gender, it is generally the same factors that explain and predict beliefs in a radical theory such as the Jews started World War II and a more mainstream theory such as one of the COVID-19 conspiracies.

4.3.5 Lebanon

For Lebanon, the results do not follow the four previous countries. Rather than seeing a battery of explanatory factors, the finding that sticks out the most is that few of our explanatory variables explain beliefs in conspiracy theories. In fact, only two factors seem to influence respondents' likelihood to believe in conspiracy theories: populist attitudes and the need for cognitive closure. Both seem to trigger an increased propensity to belief in the various conspiracy theories (see Table 5). Yet, even for these mostly statistically significant variables, the effect size appears smaller than for Canada, or Australia (e.g., the predicted effect for populist attitudes on conspiracy beliefs is less than one point for most models). Pertaining to some of the other variables, there are also some interesting nuances. Most interestingly, the effect of economic status varies significantly. High economic status triggers an increased likelihood to believe in the theory that Bill Gates and George Soros are responsible for the onset of the COVID-19 pandemic, whereas it decreases the respondents' propensity to believe that the Beirut explosion was not an accident.

Interestingly, the regression models also have poor model fit. All models in Table 6 explain less than 10 percent of the variance in the any of the five

Table 5 Determinants of Beliefs in Various Conspiracy Theories in Germany

	Climate Change	Pandemic Communism	Jews and WW2	Hitler Alive After 1945	Big Pharma Pandemic	NATO Operations
(Intercept)	1.771***	1.480***	1.648***	1.119***	1.925***	1.345***
	(0.351)	(0.367)	(0.327)	(0.337)	(0.408)	(0.343)
Age	−0.008**	−0.012***	−0.007**	−0.013***	−0.011***	−0.006*
	(0.003)	(0.003)	(0.002)	(0.002)	(0.003)	(0.003)
Gender	−0.141+	−0.164*	−0.070	0.085	−0.193*	−0.126+
	(0.077)	(0.080)	(0.072)	(0.074)	(0.089)	(0.075)
Education	−0.153**	−0.127**	−0.107*	−0.106*	−0.177**	−0.196***
	(0.047)	(0.049)	(0.044)	(0.045)	(0.055)	(0.046)
Urban/Rural	0.060+	−0.006	−0.007	0.011	0.004	−0.007
	(0.030)	(0.032)	(0.028)	(0.029)	(0.035)	(0.030)
Economic Status	0.105	−0.034	0.108	0.112	0.017	0.168*
	(0.074)	(0.077)	(0.069)	(0.070)	(0.085)	(0.072)
Political Ideology	0.089***	0.130***	0.079***	0.109***	0.077***	0.087***
	(0.018)	(0.019)	(0.017)	(0.018)	(0.021)	(0.018)
Political Interest	−0.014	−0.033*	−0.035**	−0.039**	−0.007	−0.035*
	(0.014)	(0.014)	(0.013)	(0.013)	(0.016)	(0.014)

SWD	−0.038**	−0.052***	−0.005	0.006	−0.123***	−0.004
	(0.013)	(0.014)	(0.013)	(0.013)	(0.016)	(0.013)
Populist Attitudes	0.238***	0.397***	0.136**	0.209***	0.491***	0.280***
	(0.053)	(0.055)	(0.050)	(0.051)	(0.062)	(0.052)
Religiosity	0.237**	0.245**	0.116+	0.221**	0.007	0.260***
	(0.075)	(0.078)	(0.070)	(0.072)	(0.087)	(0.073)
Need for Closure	−0.146*	−0.094	−0.070	−0.038	−0.057	−0.047
	(0.062)	(0.065)	(0.058)	(0.060)	(0.072)	(0.061)
Self-Esteem	−0.405***	−0.246***	−0.394***	−0.301***	−0.228**	−0.350***
	(0.061)	(0.064)	(0.057)	(0.058)	(0.071)	(0.060)
N	808	810	811	808	810	807
R^2	0.232	0.284	0.179	0.209	0.314	0.214
Log Likelihood	−1140.406	−1177.974	−1089.979	−1104.211	−1265.411	−1121.433
RMSE	0.99	1.04	0.93	0.95	1.15	0.97

+ $p < 0.1$, * $p < 0.05$, ** $p < 0.01$, *** $p < 0.001$

Table 6 Determinants of Beliefs in Various Conspiracy Theories in Lebanon

	Gates and Soros Pandemic	Climate Change	Pandemic Communism	Beirut Explosion Attack	Hariri & Beirut Explosion
(Intercept)	−0.529	1.011*	0.163	0.918+	0.431
	(0.436)	(0.435)	(0.493)	(0.492)	(0.450)
Age	0.003	−0.002	0.008	0.003	−0.002
	(0.005)	(0.005)	(0.005)	(0.005)	(0.005)
Gender	−0.031	0.064	0.207+	0.007	0.193+
	(0.103)	(0.103)	(0.117)	(0.116)	(0.106)
Education	0.006	−0.068	−0.116+	−0.035	−0.048
	(0.053)	(0.054)	(0.061)	(0.060)	(0.055)
Urban/Rural	0.022	0.000	0.011	0.009	0.023
	(0.039)	(0.039)	(0.044)	(0.044)	(0.040)
Economic Status	0.178+	0.009	0.251*	−0.349***	−0.171+
	(0.092)	(0.092)	(0.104)	(0.103)	(0.095)
Political Ideology	0.027	−0.003	0.019	0.015	0.019
	(0.022)	(0.022)	(0.025)	(0.025)	(0.023)
Political Interest	0.002	−0.035*	−0.024	−0.011	0.010
	(0.016)	(0.016)	(0.018)	(0.017)	(0.016)

SWD	−0.023	0.014	−0.023	0.031	0.030
	(0.020)	(0.020)	(0.022)	(0.022)	(0.020)
Populist Attitudes	0.237***	0.149*	0.258**	0.182*	0.168*
	(0.071)	(0.071)	(0.080)	(0.080)	(0.073)
Religiosity	−0.042	0.036	0.075	0.030	−0.009
	(0.096)	(0.097)	(0.109)	(0.108)	(0.100)
Need for Closure	0.367***	0.164*	0.037	0.252**	0.282***
	(0.080)	(0.081)	(0.091)	(0.091)	(0.083)
Self-Esteem	0.148+	−0.006	0.044	0.019	−0.113
	(0.080)	(0.080)	(0.091)	(0.090)	(0.083)
N	530	530	529	528	530
R^2	0.129	0.043	0.057	0.072	0.075
Log Likelihood	−776.82	−778.75	−843.10	−834.87	−796.09
RMSE	1.05	1.05	1.19	1.18	1.09

+ p < 0.1, * p < 0.05, ** p < 0.01, *** p < 0.001

conspiracy theories. This feature, coupled with the few statistically significant variables, allows us to conclude that we cannot generalize across the space when detecting the prototypical believer in conspiracy theories. The poor model fit and the many nonsignificant explanatory factors also hint at the possibility of omitted variables such as ethnicity, which might explain beliefs in conspiracy theories in this Middle Eastern country.

4.3.6 Morocco

Interestingly, the findings for Morocco closely resemble those for Lebanon in that few independent variables appear to influence belief patterns in any of the four global conspiracy theories. Again, the only two factors that seem to matter are populist attitudes and low self-esteem, even if the latter does not seem to have a statistically significant influence in all models. What also runs through all models is the low model fit. Depending on the type of conspiracy theory, all models only explain between 5 and 12 percent of the variance in conspiracy theory beliefs. Some nuance for Morocco, which appears interesting to mention, is that women and urban dwellers appear to have a somewhat higher likelihood to believe in some of the COVID-19 conspiracy theories. Even if the substantive influence of gender is quite low (e.g., women merely seem to have a .3 point higher predicted likelihood on the 5-point Likert scale to believe in some of the COVID-19 conspiracies), this finding goes against the general wisdom. More broadly the regression models in Table 7 seem to confirm that the general picture we can draw of the prototypical believer in conspiracy theories from the Western World and Brazil does not seem to apply to North Africa. In Morocco and Lebanon, there are likely other factors at stage, which the literature has not theorized.

4.3.7 South Africa

The regression results for South Africa resemble in part those of the three Western Democracies discussed previously and in part those of our two North African countries. For sure, there are some commonalities with the Western countries and Brazil. These are the negative relationship between age and conspiracy theory beliefs, the increased likelihood of individuals with populist attitudes to believe in conspiracy theories, and the role of lower self-esteem (see Table 8). However, political ideology, satisfaction with democracy, and religiosity do not appear to play any role in this African country. Interestingly, we also see some nuance pertaining to some of the other variables included in our analyses. Probably most relevant, and this is in line with some of the findings for Morocco, women appear to be more likely to believe in some scientific and medically related conspiracies

Table 7 Determinants of Beliefs in Various Conspiracy Theories Morocco

	Climate Change	Pandemic Communism	Gates and Soros COVID	Big Pharma Pandemic
(Intercept)	1.164**	0.368	-0.375	-0.375
	(0.434)	(0.413)	(0.526)	(0.526)
Age	0.004	-0.005	0.003	0.003
	(0.004)	(0.003)	(0.004)	(0.004)
Gender	-0.103	0.094	0.317**	0.317**
	(0.091)	(0.088)	(0.111)	(0.111)
Education	-0.049	0.023	0.047	0.047
	(0.053)	(0.051)	(0.065)	(0.065)
Urban/Rural	0.024	0.021	0.144*	0.144*
	(0.049)	(0.047)	(0.060)	(0.060)
Economic Status	0.069	-0.035	0.171	0.171
	(0.107)	(0.103)	(0.131)	(0.131)
Political Ideology	0.021	-0.019	0.032	0.032
	(0.019)	(0.019)	(0.024)	(0.024)
Political Interest	0.002	0.013	-0.027	-0.027
	(0.015)	(0.015)	(0.019)	(0.019)
SWD	-0.010	-0.039*	-0.024	-0.024

Table 7 (cont.)

	Climate Change	Pandemic Communism	Gates and Soros COVID	Big Pharma Pandemic
	(0.016)	(0.016)	(0.020)	(0.020)
Populist Attitudes	0.153*	0.334***	0.207**	0.207**
	(0.061)	(0.059)	(0.075)	(0.075)
Religiosity	0.071	0.273*	0.123	0.123
	(0.115)	(0.111)	(0.142)	(0.142)
Need for Closure	0.046	0.128+	0.175+	0.175+
	(0.078)	(0.075)	(0.095)	(0.095)
Self-Esteem	−0.319***	−0.050	−0.274**	−0.274**
	(0.080)	(0.077)	(0.097)	(0.097)
N	619	618	616	620
R²	0.051	0.119	0.079	0.132
Log Likelihood	−901.251	−874.298	−1018.864	−951.101
RMSE	1.04	1.00	1.26	1.12

+ p < 0.1, * p < 0.05, ** p < 0.01, *** p < 0.001

Table 8 Determinants of Beliefs in Various Conspiracy Theories in South Africa

	Climate Change	Pandemic Communism	AIDS Plan Kill Black	Birth Control Blacks	Big Pharma Pandemic	AIDS Cure Not Shared	Gates/Soros Conspiracy
(Intercept)	0.900+	1.375**	0.797	0.822+	1.010+	1.738***	0.698
	(0.489)	(0.504)	(0.499)	(0.477)	(0.522)	(0.506)	(0.481)
Age	−0.007*	−0.017***	−0.027***	−0.017***	−0.012**	−0.029***	−0.011***
	(0.003)	(0.004)	(0.004)	(0.003)	(0.004)	(0.004)	(0.003)
Gender	0.151	0.141	0.332***	0.334***	0.216*	0.262**	0.168+
	(0.094)	(0.097)	(0.096)	(0.092)	(0.101)	(0.098)	(0.093)
Education	0.066	0.028	0.162**	0.077	0.060	0.077	0.037
	(0.054)	(0.056)	(0.056)	(0.053)	(0.058)	(0.056)	(0.053)
Urban/Rural	0.058	0.047	−0.006	0.032	0.083	0.020	0.059
	(0.050)	(0.051)	(0.051)	(0.048)	(0.053)	(0.051)	(0.049)
Economic Status	−0.111	−0.142	−0.227*	−0.165+	−0.129	−0.175+	−0.107
	(0.103)	(0.106)	(0.105)	(0.100)	(0.109)	(0.106)	(0.101)
Political Ideology	0.016	0.004	0.005	0.048*	0.010	0.014	0.030
	(0.020)	(0.020)	(0.020)	(0.019)	(0.021)	(0.021)	(0.020)
Political Interest	−0.017	−0.017	0.018	−0.003	−0.013	−0.016	−0.030+

Table 8 (cont.)

	Climate Change	Pandemic Communism	AIDS Plan Kill Black	Birth Control Blacks	Big Pharma Pandemic	AIDS Cure Not Shared	Gates/Soros Conspiracy
	(0.017)	(0.017)	(0.017)	(0.016)	(0.018)	(0.017)	(0.017)
SWD	0.010	0.004	0.018	0.034*	-0.004	-0.012	0.043*
	(0.017)	(0.018)	(0.018)	(0.017)	(0.019)	(0.018)	(0.017)
Populist Attitudes	0.307***	0.295***	0.269***	0.177*	0.296***	0.377***	0.179*
	(0.078)	(0.081)	(0.080)	(0.077)	(0.084)	(0.081)	(0.077)
Religiosity	0.021	0.060	-0.174	-0.014	-0.101	0.108	0.097
	(0.115)	(0.119)	(0.118)	(0.113)	(0.123)	(0.119)	(0.113)
Need for Closure	0.054	0.175*	0.075	0.083	0.173*	0.101	0.151+
	(0.082)	(0.084)	(0.084)	(0.080)	(0.087)	(0.085)	(0.081)
Self-Esteem	-0.452***	-0.364***	-0.190*	-0.369***	-0.370***	-0.358***	-0.373***
	(0.087)	(0.089)	(0.088)	(0.085)	(0.092)	(0.090)	(0.085)
N	750	747	746	749	748	749	745
R^2	0.081	0.101	0.149	0.126	0.088	0.166	0.092
Log Likelihood	-1231.06	-1245.82	-1237.73	-1211.90	-1273.24	-1254.62	-1270.31
RMSE	1.25	1.28	1.27	1.22	1.33	1.29	1.22

+ p < 0.1, * p < 0.05, ** p < 0.01, *** p < 0.001

(e.g., AIDS was created by white people to kill Black people, and birth control and condoms were created to control the Black population and should not be used).

Like the regression models for Lebanon and Morocco, the models for South Africa have relatively low model fit. This entails that there are probably some missing variables. Given the Apartheid history and the suspicion of parts of the Black population toward science, an important variable to look at should be race (even if much of the population is Black), and possibly traditional kinship networks, which are still present in some part of the country including urban areas (Pillay 2020).

4.3.8 United States

The picture we get for the United States resembles again that of the three other Western countries. As for Australia, Canada, and Germany, the typical conspiracy believer is likely to be younger, to the right of the political spectrum, embraces populist attitudes, and has low self-esteem. Religiosity and satisfaction with democracy are also in the expected direction in five or four of the six models, respectively (see Table 9).

There is also an interesting commonality with Canada. Analogous to the Pierre Poilievre conspiracy theory, the Truther conspiracy, even if it is originally a left-wing conspiracy theory directed against President Bush, triggers more support in our survey from people who identify as right-wing. Another interesting result worth reporting for the United States is the finding that education seems to reduce individuals' propensity to reject climate change but does not seem to have any influence on the other five conspiracy theories.

4.4 Conspiracy Believers: The Comparative Picture

The final question we want to tackle in this section is: is there a systematic structure in the individual-level determinants of conspiracy theory beliefs? If so, we want to know if the same factors explain beliefs in distinct conspiracy theories not only within the same country context but also across different countries. First, we find that within each country, the believer one conspiracy theory strongly resembles that of the believer of another conspiracy theory (see Tables 2–9). In other words, in each of the eight countries, there is very little variation in the constituents of conspiracy theory belief between any of the conspiracy theories we cover. Regardless, if it is a global conspiracy theory or a local one, if it is a more widespread or niche theory, the same factors explain why some people have a higher likelihood than others to believe in any of these theories. This also implies that we find little support for partisan cheerleading,

Table 9 Determinants of Beliefs in Various Conspiracy Theories in the United States

	Climate Change	Pandemic Communism	9/11 Govt Involved	2020 Results Illegitimate	Obama Birther	Big Pharma Pandemic
(Intercept)	1.703***	1.166***	2.106***	0.970**	1.161***	1.460***
	(0.319)	(0.313)	(0.326)	(0.337)	(0.309)	(0.312)
Age	−0.018***	−0.011***	−0.021***	−0.017***	−0.010**	−0.019***
	(0.003)	(0.003)	(0.003)	(0.003)	(0.003)	(0.003)
Gender	0.006	0.073	0.019	0.128	0.025	−0.068
	(0.088)	(0.086)	(0.090)	(0.093)	(0.085)	(0.086)
Education	−0.123**	−0.080+	−0.055	−0.055	−0.033	−0.028
	(0.043)	(0.042)	(0.044)	(0.046)	(0.042)	(0.042)
Urban/Rural	−0.028	0.016	−0.056	0.101*	0.013	0.000
	(0.038)	(0.037)	(0.038)	(0.040)	(0.036)	(0.037)
Economic Status	0.126	0.019	0.132	0.116	0.095	0.009
	(0.082)	(0.081)	(0.084)	(0.087)	(0.079)	(0.080)
Political Ideology	0.143***	0.182***	0.077***	0.221***	0.213***	0.155***
	(0.017)	(0.016)	(0.017)	(0.018)	(0.016)	(0.016)
Political Interest	−0.006	0.016	0.002	−0.010	−0.007	−0.004
	(0.015)	(0.015)	(0.015)	(0.016)	(0.015)	(0.015)

SWD	−0.012	−0.081***	−0.020	−0.067***	−0.053***	−0.044**
	(0.015)	(0.015)	(0.016)	(0.016)	(0.015)	(0.015)
Populist Attitudes	0.163**	0.217***	0.291***	0.144*	0.033	0.285***
	(0.060)	(0.059)	(0.061)	(0.064)	(0.058)	(0.059)
Religiosity	0.187*	0.147+	0.038	0.262**	0.198*	0.210*
	(0.087)	(0.085)	(0.089)	(0.092)	(0.084)	(0.085)
Need for Closure	0.006	0.014	−0.034	0.012	0.021	−0.025
	(0.070)	(0.069)	(0.072)	(0.074)	(0.068)	(0.069)
Self-Esteem	−0.314***	−0.165*	−0.387***	−0.169*	−0.233***	−0.273***
	(0.072)	(0.071)	(0.074)	(0.076)	(0.070)	(0.071)
N	827	829	825	827	829	828
R^2	0.243	0.252	0.210	0.293	0.277	0.264
Log Likelihood	−1299.88	−1289.78	−1314.49	−1347.86	−1279.59	−1287.54
RMSE	1.17	1.15	1.19	1.23	1.13	1.15

+ $p < 0.1$, * $p < 0.05$, ** $p < 0.01$, *** $p < 0.001$

which refers to supporting a conspiracy theory because one's preferred party propagates it (Bullock and Lenz 2019; Prior et al. 2015). If partisan cheer-leading was an issue, we would not find the same people to support the Birther and the Truther conspiracy in the United States or an anti-Trudeau and anti-Poilievre conspiracy theory in Canada. Interestingly, we also find strong pair-wise correlations between beliefs in all specific conspiracies in most countries (see the correlation table for specific conspiracy theories in the appendix), which further supports the notion that people who believe in one conspiracy theory are also more likely to believe in another one.

However, between countries the situation is a bit more nuanced. In the Western world, and a little less so for Brazil, we find support that the factors accounting for someone to believe in conspiracy theories travel from one country to the next; that is, in each of the four Western countries we find a very homogeneous picture of belief patterns in distinct conspiracy theories (see Table 10, which summarizes the findings from each study). It seems that people who believe in one conspiracy theory also have a higher tendency to believe in another one. For Australia, Canada, Germany, and the United States, the typical conspiracy believer is younger, to the right of the political spectrum, dissatisfied with the functioning of democracy, embraces populist attitudes, self-identifies as right-wing, and has low self-esteem. These factors increase somebody's likelihood to believe in conspiracy theories, regardless of the type of theory. The characteristics of the typical believer do not change if we look at global conspiracy theories such as the COVID-19 or the climate change ones, left-wing and right-wing theories, or popular and more niche conspiracy theor-ies. For Brazil, we also find the same factors do matter, except for age.

If we look at our three African countries, Lebanon, Morocco, and South Africa, we see some divergence from the Western model. The constituents of conspiracy theory beliefs are not the same in South Africa and even more so, Lebanon, as well as Morocco, compared to our five other cases. Interestingly, Lebanon, Morocco, and South Africa join the Western world and Brazil in that there is a homogeneous belief patterns for the various conspiracy theories we asked in the three country contexts. Yet, the prototypical conspiracy believer in Lebanon, Morocco, and South Africa does not resemble the prototypical con-spiracy theory believer in the other five cases. Many of the factors which are statistically significant in the Western world appear to lose their significance in the developing world. This applies particularly to Lebanon, where the only statistically significant factor that travels is populist attitudes. We also find a new factor to be relevant in Lebanon, and this factor is the need for closure. For Morocco, the only statistically significant variables appear to be populist attitudes and to a lesser degree a lack of self-esteem, which is not significant in

Table 10 Summary of the Findings by Country

	Australia	Brazil	Canada	Germany	Lebanon	Morocco	South Africa	United States
Age	(−)	n.s.	(−)	(−)	n.s.	n.s.	(−)	(−)
Gender	n.s.	n.s.	n.s.	n.s.	n.s.	(+)	(+)	n.s.
Education	n.s.	(−)	(−)	(−)	n.s.	n.s.	n.s.	n.s.
Urban/Rural	n.s.	n.s.	n.s.	n.s.	n.s.	n.s.	n.s.	n.s.
Economic Status	n.s.	n.s.	n.s.	n.s.	n.s.	n.s.	n.s.	n.s.
Political Ideology	(+)	(+)	(+)	(+)	n.s.	n.s.	(+)	(+)
Political Interest	n.s.	n.s.	n.s.	(−)	n.s.	n.s.	n.s.	n.s.
SWD	(−)	n.s.	(−)	(−)	n.s.	n.s.	n.s.	(−)
Populist Attitudes	(+)	(+)	(+)	(+)	(+)	(+)	(+)	(+)
Religiosity	(+)	n.s.	(+)	(+)	n.s.	n.s.	n.s.	(+)
Need for Closure	n.s.	n.s.	n.s.	n.s.	(+)	n.s.	n.s.	n.s.
Self-Esteem	(−)	(−)	(−)	(−)	n.s.	(−)	(−)	(−)

Note. (−) or (+) identifies the variable had a significant (+ for positive and − for negative) relationship for a majority of the conspiracy theories tested in that country; *n.s.* indicates the relationship was not significant.

all models. The other indicators lose their significance. For South Africa, the differences in belief pattern with the Western countries are less pronounced. In this sub-Saharan country, our results illustrate three of the original six statistically significant variables keep their relevancy. These are age, populist attitudes, and low self-esteem. However, the other three (i.e., religiosity, satisfaction with democracy, and right-wing ideology) lose their statistical significance in this Africa country. Altogether, this allows for the tentative conclusion – that there is indeed a standard or prototypical conspiracy theory believer in the Western World, and to a lesser degree Brazil. Within the same country context and across countries this prototypical believer does not change. However, if we move to Africa and the Middle East many of the statistically significant variables lose their influence, and we cannot generalize any more, even if the internal picture within each of the three African/ Middle Eastern countries we study remains homogeneous.

5 Conclusion and Implications

5.1 Conspiracy Theories through a Comparative Lens

This Element provides a nice introduction into conspiracy theories in different contexts and presents the characteristics of the people who believe in such theories. Some of the contributions are descriptive in nature, while others are analytical. Descriptively, we have presented contemporary conspiracy theories. These include global conspiracy theories, which exist in literally every corner of the world. Climate change denial or a host of COVID-19-related conspiracies are examples of such global conspiracy theories. In addition, we have introduced country-specific conspiracies, which sometimes also spread and adapt to other contexts. An example could be QAnon and its offsprings in Australia and Germany. The Big Lie, which originated in the United States and then spread to Brazil, would be another example. A third group of conspiracy theories is purely home-made and contextualizes a domestic event. The Trudeau or Poilievre conspiracies in Canada would be examples.

What all these conspiracy theories have in common is that they target elites. Nevertheless, the specific target can be distinct. Some conspiracies target governments (i.e., the Chinese government in the case of the Australian prime minister Holt conspiracy theory), while others target financial institutions or important business personalities (e.g., George Soros and Bill Gates are presented as the initiators of COVID-19). A third group targets science or medical science (e.g., several of the South Africa conspiracy theories). In addition, there are race-based conspiracy theories (e.g., the Jews are responsible the onset of World War II) or politically inspired ones that target political opponents (e.g. these are directed against a political leader such as President Bush or Prime Minister Trudeau).

The second contribution is also descriptive. We provide an illustration of the number of people who believe in conspiracy theories. We find that in every country millions of people believe in them. Of course, the number of believers can strongly vary from one conspiracy theory to the next. However, even very radical conspiracy theories such as the one that affirms that Hitler did not die and lived to old age still trigger the support of 5 or more percent of the German population. More popular ones such as the COVID-19 conspiracies or some domestic theories such as the Big Lie garner 20, 25, and sometimes over 30 percent of support among the respective national populations. It is concerning to say the least, if one-fifth to one-third of the population live in an alternative environment, where fiction becomes truth and truth becomes fiction. As the current situation of the United States highlights, this can put tremendous pressure on democratic institutions.

A third descriptive contribution, which the literature has not discussed prominently refers to the high percentage of citizens, who classify themselves in the do not know or uncertain category. Across the different types of conspiracy theories and across the eight countries, we find that roughly between 15 and 30 percent choose the answer uncertain with even higher numbers for Morocco and Lebanon. Here is the question that arises from this tendency: Are respondents uncertain about the truth of the conspiracy statement or do they choose the middle category out of convenience?

The answer to this question is very relevant for our understanding of conspiracy theories and their spread. To illustrate, it would be disturbing if nearly 21 percent of Germans are uncertain about the statement whether the Jews were responsible for starting World War II, even more so because World War II is probably the most taught subject in history classes in school. For future research, it would be interesting to reduce the five-item Likert Scale to measure conspiracy theories to a four-item Likert Scale. Will those in the uncertain category rather move to the true or the false category? More qualitatively, it would be interesting to open the black box of this one-fifth to one-third of respondents (or half of the respondents in Lebanon and Morocco for some theories), who have chosen the answer uncertain and ask them more qualitatively why they have chosen the middle category.

The fourth contribution is more inferential. Looking at the determinants of conspiracy theory belief, we find that there is one indicator – populist attitudes – that seems to trigger an increased probability to believe in conspiracy theories regardless of context. In other words, individuals who embrace peoples' centrism and anti-elitism, as well as who have a Manichean perspective of the world that identifies good and evil, also appear to have a higher likelihood to believe in conspiracy theories. In fact, conspiracy theories use the ingredients of populism to construct alternative, untrue, or unconfirmed narratives of often tragic events, narratives that clearly identify a culprit (i.e., vicious elites) for these sinister events. Regardless of the context, this symbiosis between the two concepts likely contributes to the tendency of individuals with populist attitudes to also have a higher likelihood to believe in conspiracy theories.

Aside from populist attitudes, we do not find support in our regression analysis of other factors that could explain conspiratorial beliefs across the eight country contexts. However, this does not mean that we do not find support for the ideal of a systematic structure in the individual-level determinants of conspiracy theory beliefs. Rather, our models portray strong homogeneity in the factors that trigger conspiratorial beliefs within each of the eight cases. In other words, in each country the belief patterns in one conspiracy theory seem to mimic the belief patterns in another one. Probably, even more importantly, our results illustrate that there appear to be few differences in the typical conspiracy believer across our four Western countries and Brazil. Such a person appears to share six attributes. He/she is likely to be younger, religious, to the right of the political spectrum, dissatisfied with the government, embracing populist attitudes, and with low self-system. For Brazil the only factor that does not seem to apply is age. These same attributes appear to explain international conspiracies, domestic conspiracies, left- and right-wing, as well as niche and more mainstream theories.

For the non-Western countries, fewer factors seem relevant. For South Africa, we only find that three factors appear to consistently influence citizens' beliefs in the six conspiracies we have selected. These variables are age, populist attitudes, and self-esteem. For Lebanon, it is only two indicators (i.e., populist attitudes and need for closure). The same applies to Morocco, where populist attitudes and low self-esteem seem to largely account for someone's higher or lower likelihood to believe in conspiracy theories. The models for South Africa, Lebanon, and Morocco also have lower model fit, which might open the possibility that other variables such as race or kinship networks play a role there. Future research should look more into non-Western contexts and explain the constituents of conspiracy theories. This includes the intriguing question why some of the factors such as religiosity or dissatisfaction with democracy do not seem to play a role in most non-Western countries, or at least in three out of the four countries we studied. More broadly, future research could include other factors such as authoritarian values or Narcissism, which could also trigger increased beliefs in conspiracy theories.

Fifth and this is also a more analytical contribution. We find that several variables we have included appear to have no influence. Except for age, which except for Lebanon and Morocco tends to display a consistent negative influence, we find that most demographics and several socioeconomic indicators do not seem to have any bearing when it comes to explaining beliefs in conspiracy theories. These include education, income status, gender, place of residency, and political interest. This further implies that beliefs in conspiracy theories do not appear to be restricted to a specific social class. Rather, conspiracy theories appear to have reached the center of society; they seem to reach upward 30 percent of citizens, and this includes educated and noneducated individuals, men and women, rich and poor people, citizens, who live on the countryside and in cities, as well as politically interested and non-interested people. Another important finding revolves around the noneffect of political interest. Conspiracy theories do not seem to be a unique feature of the politically alienated, who know little to nothing about politics; they also appear to spread among politically engaged individuals, especially those who are engaged in right-wing groups. Making at least five contributions to our understanding of conspiracy theory beliefs, we hope that this Element provides a comprehensive introduction to conspiracy theories. It hopefully familiarizes the reader with the main theories, provides a snapshot of the popularity of these theories, and presents the typical conspiracy theory believer. However, we also see the need for more truly comparative research given that there is no country in the world which does not grapple with conspiracy theories. Future work should include conspiracy theories and their believers in Asia, Latin America, or Eastern Europe. In this sense, we hope that this Element constitutes a beginning rather than an end. It should be a beginning into a truly comparative research agenda that reaches beyond the Western world and that compares/contrasts and analyzes conspiracy theories and their believers in any corner of the world.

References

Abadi J (2020) Perception and reality in US-Lebanon relations. *Middle Eastern Studies* 56(2), 305–326.

Abalakina-Paap M, Stephan WG, Craig T and Gregory WL (1999) Beliefs in conspiracies. *Political Psychology* 20(3), 637–647.

Adam H and Moodley K (2023) *The opening of the Apartheid mind: Options for the new South Africa*. University of California Press.

Akkerman A, Mudde C and Zaslove A (2014) How populist are the people? Measuring populist attitudes in voters. *Comparative Political Studies* 47(9), 1324–1353.

Al-Wutayd O, Khalil R and Rajar AB (2021) Sociodemographic and behavioral predictors of COVID-19 vaccine hesitancy in Pakistan. *Journal of Multidisciplinary Healthcare*, 14, 2847–2856.

Albaghli B and Carlucci L (2021) The link between Muslim religiosity and negative attitudes toward the West: An Arab study. *The International Journal for the Psychology of Religion* 31(4), 235–248.

Alcorn G (2016) The Reality of Safe Schools. www.theguardian.com/australia-news/2016/dec/14/safe-schools-roz-ward-life-saving-support-queer-theory-classroom (accessed June 23, 2023).

Anti-Defamation League (2020) Coronavirus: Prominent Conspiracies. www.adl.org/resources/blog/coronavirus-prominent-conspiracies (accessed December 29, 2022).

Arceneaux K and Truex R (2023) Donald Trump and the lie. *Perspectives on Politics* 21(3), 863–879. https://doi.org/10.1017/S1537592722000901.

Architecture F (2020) The Beirut Port Explosion (Arabic). In Youtube.

Arnold GB (2008) Conspiracy theory in film, television, and politics. http://digital.casalini.it/9781567207224; ISBN: 9781567207224.

Badham V (2021) Qanon: How the Far-Right Cult Took Australians Down a "Rabbit Hole" of Extremism. *The Guardian*.

Bago B, Rand DG and Pennycook G (2022) Does deliberation decrease belief in conspiracies? *Journal of Experimental Social Psychology* 103, 104395.

Baker SA and Maddox A (2022) From COVID-19 treatment to miracle cure: The role of influencers and public figures in amplifying the hydroxychloroquine and ivermectin conspiracy theories during the pandemic. *M/C Journal* 25(1).

Bantimaroudis P (2016) Chemtrails in the sky: Toward a group-mediated delusion theory. *Studies in Media and Communication* 4(2), 23–31.

Bastos M and Recuero R (2023) The insurrectionist playbook: Jair Bolsonaro and the National Congress of Brazil. *Social Media+ Society* 9(4), 20563051231211881.

Baumann H (2016) *Citizen Hariri: Lebanon's neoliberal reconstruction.* Oxford University Press.

Baumeister RF, Campbell JD, Krueger JI and Vohs KD (2005) Exploding the self-esteem myth. *Scientific American* 292(1), 84–91.

Begley L (2009) *Why the Dreyfus affair matters.* Yale University Press.

Bell L (2011) *Climate of corruption: Politics and power behind the global warming hoax.* Greenleaf Book Group.

Bennhold K (2020) QAnon is thriving in Germany: The extreme right is delighted. *The New York Times* 11, 2020.

Bernardi C (2015) Getting to the Bottom of the Halal Certification Racket. [Blog] March 25. www.corybernardi.com/getting_to_the_bottom_of_the_halal_certification_racket.

Bertrand N, Brown P, Williams KB and Cohen Z (2021) Senior Biden Officials Finding that Covid Lab Leak Theory as Credible as Natural Origins Explanation. www.cnn.com/2021/07/16/politics/biden-intel-review-covid-origins/index.html (accessed December 25, 2022).

Bierwiaczonek K, Kunst JR and Pich O (2020) Belief in COVID-19 conspiracy theories reduces social distancing over time. *Applied Psychology: Health and Well-Being* 12(4), 1270–1285.

Birchall C and Knight P (2022) Do your own research: Conspiracy theories and the Internet. *Social Research: An International Quarterly* 89(3), 579–605.

Bloom M and Moskalenko S (2022) QAnon, women, and the American culture wars. *Social Research: An International Quarterly* 89(3), 525–550.

Blundell D (2023) What Are the Chances Pierre Poilievre Is a Foreign Asset? Pretty Good, Actually . . . . https://crier.co/2/ (accessed January 29, 2024).

Bordeleau J-N (2023) I trends: A review of conspiracy theory research: Definitions, trends, and directions for future research. *International Political Science Abstracts* 73(1), 1–10. https://doi.org/10.1177/00208345231157664.

Bordeleau J-N and Stockemer D (2024) On the relationship between age and conspiracy beliefs. *Political Psychology*, 1–16. https://doi.org/10.1111/pops.13044.

Bordeleau J-N, Stockemer D, Amengay A and Shamaileh A (2023) The comparative conspiracy research survey (CCRS): A new cross-national dataset for the study of conspiracy beliefs. *European Political Science*, 1–11.

Brotherton R (2015) *Suspicious minds: Why we believe conspiracy theories.* Bloomsbury.

Bruder M, Haffke P, Neave N, Nouripanah N and Imhoff R (2013) Measuring individual differences in generic beliefs in conspiracy theories across cultures: Conspiracy mentality questionnaire. *Frontiers in Psychology* 4, 225.

Brüggemann M, Elgesem D, Bienzeisler N, Gertz HD and Walter S (2020) Mutual group polarization in the blogosphere: Tracking the hoax discourse on climate change. *International Journal of Communication* 14, 24.

Bullock JG and Lenz G (2019) Partisan bias in surveys. *Annual Review of Political Science* 22(1), 325–342.

Burni A, Stockemer D and Hackenesch C (2023) Contagious politics and COVID-19: Does the infectious disease hit populist supporters harder? *Contemporary Politics* 29(4), 466–491.

Busbridge R, Moffitt B and Thorburn J (2020) Cultural Marxism: Far-right conspiracy theory in Australia's culture wars. *Social Identities* 26(6), 722–738.

Butter M and Knight P (2019) The history of conspiracy theory research: A review and commentary, In Uscinski JE (ed.), *Conspiracy theories and the people who believe them*. Oxford Academic. https://doi.org/10.1093/oso/9780190844073.003.0002.

Byford J (2011) *Conspiracy theories: A critical introduction*. Springer.

Byler D and Woodsome K (2021) Opinion: False, Toxic Sept. 11 Conspiracy Theories Are Still Widespread Today. *Washington Post*.

Cairns R (2016) Climates of suspicion: "Chemtrail" conspiracy narratives and the international politics of geoengineering. *The Geographical Journal* 182(1), 70–84.

Calfano BR (2020) Government-corroborated conspiracies: Motivating response to (and belief in) a coordinated crime. *PS: Political Science & Politics* 53(1), 64–71.

Carey M (2017) *Mistrust: An ethnographic theory*. Hau Books.

Casara BGS, Suitner C and Jetten J (2022) The impact of economic inequality on conspiracy beliefs. *Journal of Experimental Social Psychology* 98, 104245.

Cassese EC, Farhart CE and Miller JM (2020) Gender differences in COVID-19 conspiracy theory beliefs. *Politics & Gender* 16(4), 1009–1018.

Chaara A (2021) Beliefs of Moroccans facing the COVID-19. *SAS Journal of Medicine* 5, 178–185.

Cheney K (2016) No, Clinton Didn't Start the Birther Thing: This Guy Did. *Politico. com*.

Christner C (2022) Populist attitudes and conspiracy beliefs: Exploring the relation between the latent structures of populist attitudes and conspiracy beliefs. *Journal of Social and Political Psychology* 10(1), 72–85.

Cichocka A, Marchlewska M and De Zavala AG (2016) Does self-love or self-hate predict conspiracy beliefs? Narcissism, self-esteem, and the endorsement of conspiracy theories. *Social Psychological and Personality Science* 7(2), 157–166.

Clifford S, Kim Y and Sullivan BW (2019) An improved question format for measuring conspiracy beliefs. *Public Opinion Quarterly* 83(4), 690–722.

Davies G, Wu E and Frank R (2023) A witch's brew of grievances: The potential effects of COVID-19 on radicalization to violent extremism. *Studies in Conflict & Terrorism* 46(11), 2327–2350.

de Graaf BA, van der Heide E, Wanmaker S and Weggemans DJ (2013) The Anders Behring Breivik Trial: Performing Justice, Defending Democracy. In *ICCT*. https://icct.nl/sites/default/files/2023-01/ICCT-De-Graaf-et-al-The-Anders-Behring-Breivik-Trial-August-2013.pdf.

de Mello ACR and Estre F (2023) Populism and anti-globalism on Twitter: Similarities of conspiratorial discourse and content diffusion on social networks in Brazil, Spain, Latin America, and Italy. In Pereira AW (ed.), *Right-wing populism in Latin America and beyond*. Routledge, 133–154.

de Sá Guimarães F, Miquelasi AF, Ferreira Alves GJ, de Oliveira e Silva IDG and Stange Calandrin K (2023) The evangelical foreign policy model: Jair Bolsonaro and evangelicals in Brazil. *Third World Quarterly* 44(6), 1324–1344.

Demuru P (2020) Conspiracy theories, messianic populism and everyday social media use in contemporary Brazil a glocal semiotic perspective. *Glocalism* 3(3), 1–42. https://doi.org/10.12893/gjcpi.2020.3.12.

Dickinson D (2013) Myths or theories? Alternative beliefs about HIV and AIDS in South African working class communities. *African Journal of AIDS Research* 12(3), 121–130.

Djuric M (2023) Poilievre's Conservative Party Embracing Language of Mainstream Conspiracy Theories. www.ctvnews.ca/politics/poilievre-s-conservative-party-embracing-language-of-mainstream-conspiracy-theories-1.6517247 (accessed January 29, 2024).

Dorfman R (1980) Conspiracy city. *Journal of Popular Film and Television* 7(4), 434–456.

Douglas KM (2021) COVID-19 conspiracy theories. *Group Processes & Intergroup Relations* 24(2), 270–275.

Douglas KM and Sutton RM (2015) Climate change: Why the conspiracy theories are dangerous. *Bulletin of the Atomic Scientists* 71(2), 98–106.

Douglas KM, Sutton RM, Jolley D and Wood MJ (2015) The social, political, environmental, and health-related consequences of conspiracy theories: Problems and potential solutions. In *The psychology of conspiracy*. Routledge, 183–200.

Douglas KM, Uscinski JE, Sutton RM et al. (2019) Understanding conspiracy theories. *Political Psychology* 40, 3–35.

Drake F (2014) *Global warming*. Routledge.

Duncan B (2001) *Crusade or conspiracy? Catholics and the anti-communist struggle in Australia*. UNSW Press.

Dyrendal A (2020) Conspiracy theory and religion. In Bilewicz M, Cichocka A, and Soral W (eds.), *Routledge handbook of conspiracy theories*. Routledge, 371–383.

El Hajj S (2021) Writing (from) the Rubble: Reflections on the August 4, 2020 explosion in Beirut, Lebanon. *Life Writing* 18(1), 7–23.

Enders A, Farhart C, Miller J et al. (2022) Are Republicans and Conservatives more likely to believe conspiracy theories? *Political Behavior*, 35, 2001–2024.

Enders AM (2019) Conspiratorial thinking and political constraint. *Public Opinion Quarterly* 83(3), 510–533.

Enders AM, Smallpage SM and Lupton RN (2020) Are all "birthers" conspiracy theorists? On the relationship between conspiratorial thinking and political orientations. *British Journal of Political Science* 50(3), 849–866.

Erisen C, Guidi M, Martini S et al. (2021) Psychological correlates of populist attitudes. *Political Psychology* 42, 149–171.

Evans RJ (2020) *The Hitler conspiracies: The protocols – the stab in the back – the Reichstag fire – Rudolf Hess – the escape from the bunker*. Oxford University Press.

Farhart CE, Douglas-Durham E, Trujillo KL and Vitriol JA (2022) Vax attacks: How conspiracy theory belief undermines vaccine support. *Progress in Molecular Biology and Translational Science* 188(1), 135–169.

Farias DBL, Casarões G and Magalhães D (2022) Radical right populism and the politics of cruelty: The case of COVID-19 in Brazil under President Bolsonaro. *Global Studies Quarterly* 2(2), ksab048.

Farokhi Z (2022) Making freedom great again: Conspiracy theories, affective nostalgia and alignment, and the right-wing base grammars of the #Freeedomconvoy. *Global Media Journal* 14(1), 67–92.

Fassin D (2007) Entre désir de nation et théorie du complot: Les idéologies du médicament en Afrique du Sud. *Sciences sociales et santé* 25(4), 93–114.

Fildebrandt D (2020) How Trudeau Bought the Media. www.westernstandard .news/features/how-trudeau-bought-the-media/article_58fdf7e6-39b9-5e78-a174-4a132b58a767.html (accessed January 29, 2024).

Foster JE and Wolfson MC (2010) Polarization and the decline of the middle class: Canada and the US. *The Journal of Economic Inequality* 8, 247–273.

Frame T (2005) The life and death of Harold Holt. *Australian Journal of Social Issues* 40(3), 461–462.

Franks B, Bangerter A and Bauer MW (2013) Conspiracy theories as quasi-religious mentality: An integrated account from cognitive science, social representations theory, and frame theory. *Frontiers in Psychology* 4, 424.

Freeman D, Waite F, Rosebrock L et al. (2022) Coronavirus conspiracy beliefs, mistrust, and compliance with government guidelines in England. *Psychological Medicine* 52(2), 251–263.

Frenken M, Bilewicz M and Imhoff R (2023) On the relation between religiosity and the endorsement of conspiracy theories: The role of political orientation. *Political Psychology* 44(1), 139–156.

Galais C and Rico G (2021) An unjustified bad reputation? The Dark Triad and support for populism. *Electoral Studies* 72, 102357.

Garry A, Walther S, Rukaya R and Mohammed A (2021) QAnon conspiracy theory: Examining its evolution and mechanisms of radicalization. *Journal for Deradicalization* 26, 152–216.

Gemenis K (2021) Explaining conspiracy beliefs and scepticism around the COVID-19 pandemic. *Swiss Political Science Review* 27(2), 229–242.

Georgiou N, Delfabbro P and Balzan R (2019) Conspiracy beliefs in the general population: The importance of psychopathology, cognitive style and educational attainment. *Personality and Individual Differences* 151, 109521.

Ghaddar A, Khandaqji S, Awad Z and Kansoun R (2022) Conspiracy beliefs and vaccination intent for COVID-19 in an infodemic. *PLoS One* 17(1), e0261559.

Gillies J, Raynauld V and Wisniewski A (2023) Canada is no exception: The 2022 freedom convoy, political entanglement, and identity-driven protest. *American Behavioral Scientist*, 00027642231166885.

Goertzel T (1994) Belief in conspiracy theories. *Political Psychology*, 15(4), 731–742.

Goreis A and Voracek M (2019) A systematic review and meta-analysis of psychological research on conspiracy beliefs: Field characteristics, measurement instruments, and associations with personality traits. *Frontiers in Psychology* 10, 205.

Grebe E and Nattrass N (2012) AIDS conspiracy beliefs and unsafe sex in Cape Town. *AIDS and Behavior* 16, 761–773.

Gruzd A, Mai P and Soares FB (2022) How coordinated link sharing behavior and partisans' narrative framing fan the spread of COVID-19 misinformation and conspiracy theories. *Social Network Analysis and Mining* 12(1), 118.

Halafoff A, Marriott E, Fitzpatrick R and Weng E (2022) Selling (con) spirituality and COVID-19 in Australia: Convictions, complexity and countering dis/misinformation. *Journal for the Academic Study of Religion* 35(2), 141–167.

Hancock J (1998) Lebanon and the west: UK, EU and US. *Mediterranean Politics* 3(1), 163–169.

Harvey LD (2018) *Global warming*. Routledge.

Haupt PI (1991) A universe of lies: Holocaust revisionism and the myth of a Jewish world-conspiracy. *Patterns of Prejudice* 25(1), 75–85.

Heilweil R (2020) How the 5G Coronavirus Conspiracy Theory Went from Fringe to Mainstream. *Vox*.

Hidalgo OF (2022) Religions and conspiracy theories as the authoritarian "other" of democracy? *Politics and Governance* 10(4), 146–156.

Hill SJ and Roberts ME (2023) Acquiescence bias inflates estimates of conspiratorial beliefs and political misperceptions. *Political Analysis* 31(4), 575–590.

Hislop M (2021) COVID-19 Style Conspiracy Theories Bedevil Alberta Oil and Gas Politics Thanks to UCP. https://energi.media/markham-on-energy/covid-19-style-conspiracy-theories-bedevil-alberta-oil-and-gas-politics-thanks-to-ucp/ (accessed November 23, 2023).

Hofstadter R (1966) The paranoid style in American politics. In Hofstadter R (ed.), *The paranoid style in American politics and other essays*. Knopf, 3–40.

Hogg R, Nkala B, Dietrich J et al. (2017) Conspiracy beliefs and knowledge about HIV origins among adolescents in Soweto, South Africa. *PLoS One* 12(2), e0165087.

Hornsey M and Pearson S (2022) Cross-national differences in willingness to believe conspiracy theories. *Current Opinion in Psychology*, 47, 101391.

Hornsey MJ, Pearson S, Kang J et al. (2023) Multinational data show that conspiracy beliefs are associated with the perception (and reality) of poor national economic performance. *European Journal of Social Psychology* 53(1), 78–89. https://doi.org/10.1002/ejsp.2888.

Imhoff R, Zimmer F, Klein O et al. (2022) Conspiracy mentality and political orientation across 26 countries. *Nature Human Behaviour* 6(3), 392–403.

Inhofe JM (2012) *The greatest hoax: How the global warming conspiracy threatens your future*. WND Books.

Jacobson GC (2023) The dimensions, origins, and consequences of belief in Donald Trump's big lie. *Political Science Quarterly* 138(2), 133–166.

Jeitler C (2021) Mainstreaming Extremism or Radicalizing the Center. www.aicgs.org/2021/11/mainstreaming-extremism-or-radicalizing-the-center/#_ftn3 (accessed December 3, 2022).

Jensen EA, Pfleger A, Herbig L et al. (2021) What drives belief in vaccination conspiracy theories in Germany? *Frontiers in Communication* 6, 678335.

Jones C (2023) "We the people, not the sheeple": QAnon and the transnational mobilisation of millennialist far-right conspiracy theories. *First Monday.* https://doi.org/10.5210/fm.v28i3.12854.

Karić T and Međedović J (2021) Covid-19 conspiracy beliefs and containment-related behaviour: The role of political trust. *Personality and Individual Differences* 175, 110697.

Kashima T (2011) *Judgment without Trial: Japanese American imprisonment during World War II.* University of Washington Press.

Keeley BL (2019) Of conspiracy theories. In Coady D (ed.), *Conspiracy theories.* Routledge, 45–60.

Khan M, Adil SF, Alkhathlan HZ et al. (2020) COVID-19: A global challenge with old history, epidemiology and progress so far. *Molecules* 26(1), 39.

Kim Y (2022) How conspiracy theories can stimulate political engagement. *Journal of Elections, Public Opinion and Parties* 32(1), 1–21.

Klein C, Clutton P and Dunn AG (2019) Pathways to conspiracy: The social and linguistic precursors of involvement in Reddit's conspiracy theory forum. *PLoS One* 14(11), e0225098.

Konopka M (2023) Understanding the Freedom Convoy Movement's Collective Identity and Roles of Conspiracy Narratives.

Kőszegi B, Loewenstein G and Murooka T (2022) Fragile self-esteem. *The Review of Economic Studies* 89(4), 2026–2060.

Kraus MW, Piff PK, Mendoza-Denton R, Rheinschmidt ML and Keltner D (2012) Social class, solipsism, and contextualism: How the rich are different from the poor. *Psychological Review* 119(3), 546.

Lahoud N (2023) The (in) effectiveness of conspiracy theories in the Arab world. *Democracy and Security* 19(4), 425–445.

Lantian A, Muller D, Nurra C and Douglas KM (2017) 'I know things they don't know!' : The role of need for uniqueness in belief in conspiracy theories. *Social Psychology* 48(3), 160–173, https://doi.org/10.1027/1864-9335/a000306.

Lantian A, Muller D, Nurra C et al. (2018) Stigmatized beliefs: Conspiracy theories, anticipated negative evaluation of the self, and fear of social exclusion. *European Journal of Social Psychology* 48(7), 939–954.

Leger (2022) The Freedom Convoy and Federal Politics – February 8, 2022. https://leger360.com/surveys/legers-north-american-tracker-february-8-2022/ (accessed January 30, 2024).

Leman PJ and Cinnirella M (2013) Beliefs in conspiracy theories and the need for cognitive closure. *Frontiers in Psychology* 4, 378.

Levant E (2021) Every News Media Who Secretly Took Trudeau's $61 M Pre-election Pay-off. www.rebelnews.com/exclusive_news_media_who_secretly_took_trudeaus_61m_pre-election_pay-off (accessed January 30, 2024).

Levitt M (2024) *Hezbollah: The global footprint of Lebanon's party of God.* Georgetown University Press.

Lewis E (2021) Why Lebanon's Vaccine Rollout Is Going Slower than Expected – but Faster than the Numbers Suggest. https://today.lorientlejour.com/article/1253360/why-lebanons-vaccine-rollout-is-going-slower-than-expected-but-faster-than-the-numbers-suggest.html (accessed January 3, 2023).

Li J, Lu M, Xia T and Guo Y (2018) Materialism as compensation for self-esteem among lower-class students. *Personality and Individual Differences* 131, 191–196.

Ling J (2021) Alberta's Petrostate Propaganda Has Turned Conspiratorial. https://foreignpolicy.com/2021/03/19/albertas-petrostate-propaganda-canada-germany/ (accessed March 19, 2021).

Lohiniva A-L, Barakat A, Dueger E, Restrepo S and El Aouad R (2014) A qualitative study of vaccine acceptability and decision making among pregnant women in Morocco during the A (H1N1) pdm09 pandemic. *PLoS One* 9(10), e96244.

MacMillen SL and Rush T (2022) QAnon – Religious roots, religious responses. *Critical Sociology* 48(6), 989–1004.

Mao JY, Yang SL and Guo YY (2020) Are individuals from lower social classes more susceptible to conspiracy theories? An explanation from the compensatory control theory. *Asian Journal of Social Psychology* 23(4), 372–383.

Marchlewska M, Cichocka A and Kossowska M (2018) Addicted to answers: Need for cognitive closure and the endorsement of conspiracy beliefs. *European Journal of Social Psychology* 48(2), 109–117.

Marcondes D and de Almeida Silva AR (2023) The role of Brazil in the Russia-Ukraine conflict: A potential peace enabler? *Journal of International Affairs* 75(2), 79–96. https://www.jstor.org/stable/27231738.

Mare A and Munoriyarwa A (2022) Guardians of truth? Fact-checking the "disinfodemic" in Southern Africa during the COVID-19 pandemic. *Journal of African Media Studies* 14(1), 63–79.

Mari S, Gil de Zúñiga H, Suerdem A et al. (2022) Conspiracy theories and institutional trust: Examining the role of uncertainty avoidance and active social media use. *Political Psychology* 43(2), 277–296.

Marques MD, Ling M, Williams MN, Kerr JR and McLennan J (2022) Australasian public awareness and belief in conspiracy theories: Motivational correlates. *Political Psychology* 43(1), 177–198.

Martin P (2001) US Planned War in Afghanistan Long before September 11. *World Socialist Web Site* 20.

Martin P (2002) Was the US Government Alerted to September 11 Attack. *World Socialist Website.*

Mazaheri N (2024) Faith in science: Religion and climate ahange attitudes in the Middle East. *Global Environmental Politics* 24(1), 52–75.

McGowan M and Walters J (2017) Trump's Call for Some "Good Old Global Warming" Ridiculed by Climate Experts. *The Guardian.*

McKenna E and O'Donnell C (2024) Satellite political movements: How grassroots activists Bolster Trump and Bolsonaro in the United States and Brazil. *American Behavioral Scientist* 68(13), 1782–1803. https://doi.org/10.1177/00027642241267939.

Meade A (2020) Andrew Bolt's Column Mocking Greta Thunberg Breached Standards, Press Watchdog Finds. www.theguardian.com/media/2020/jun/04/andrew-bolts-column-mocking-greta-thunberg-breached-standards-press-watchdog-finds (accessed November 15, 2022).

Mifdal M (2023) Post-truth, conspiracy, and fake news in the uncertain times of the COVID-19 pandemic in Morocco. *Social Science Information* 62(2), 160–183.

Miller JM, Saunders KL and Farhart CE (2016) Conspiracy endorsement as motivated reasoning: The moderating roles of political knowledge and trust. *American Journal of Political Science* 60(4), 824–844.

Min SJ (2021) Who believes in conspiracy theories? Network diversity, political discussion, and conservative conspiracy theories on social media. *American Politics Research* 49(5), 415–427.

Mitchell S (2018) Empire as accusation, denial, and structure: The social life of US power at Brazil's spaceport. In McGranahan C and Collins JF (eds.), *Ethnographies of US Empire*. Duke University Press, 369–390. https://doi.org/10.2307/j.ctv120qtmn.

Moore A (2018) Conspiracies, conspiracy theories and democracy. *Political Studies Review* 16(1), 2–12.

Muro A (2021) Lebanese Slow to Accept COVID Vaccine. https://nowlebanon.com/lebanese-slow-to-accept-covid-vaccine/ (accessed December 1, 2023).

Murphy R (2023) Rex Murphy: Liberals Come for Alberta Oil Workers with Mistitled Sustainable Jobs Act. https://nationalpost.com/opinion/liberals-come-for-alberta-oil-workers-with-mistitled-sustainable-jobs-act (accessed January 29, 2024).

Napolitano MG and Reuter K (2023) What is a conspiracy theory? *Erkenntnis* 88(5), 2035–2062.

Nattrass N (2012) The AIDS conspiracy. In *The AIDS conspiracy.* Columbia University Press.

Ntontis E, Jurstakova K, Neville F, Haslam SA and Reicher S (2024) A warrant for violence? An analysis of Donald Trump's speech before the US Capitol attack. *British Journal of Social Psychology* 63(1), 3–19.

Oliver JE and Wood TJ (2014) Conspiracy theories and the paranoid style (s) of mass opinion. *American Journal of Political Science* 58(4), 952–966.

Olmsted KS (2019) *Real enemies: Conspiracy theories and American democracy, World War I to 9/11.* Oxford University Press.

Önnerfors A and Krouwel A (2021) *Europe: Continent of conspiracies: Conspiracy theories in and about Europe.* Routledge.

Ozawa JV, Lukito J, Bailez F and Fakhouri LG (2024) Brazilian Capitol attack: The interaction between Bolsonaro's supporters' content, WhatsApp, Twitter, and news media. *Harvard Kennedy School Misinformation Review.* 5(2), 1–14.

Pacheco D (2024) Bots, elections, and controversies: Twitter insights from Brazil's polarised elections. In *Proceedings of the ACM on Web Conference 2024 (WWW '24).* Association for Computing Machinery, 2651–2659. https://doi.org/10.1145/3589334.3645651.

Partridge C (2018) Popular music, conspiracy culture, and the sacred. In Dyrendal A, Robertson DG, and Asprem E (eds.), *Handbook of conspiracy theory and contemporary religion.* Brill, 180–206.

Pasek J, Stark TH, Krosnick JA and Tompson T (2015) What motivates a conspiracy theory? Birther beliefs, partisanship, liberal-conservative ideology, and anti-Black attitudes. *Electoral Studies* 40, 482–489.

Pennycook G, McPhetres J, Bago B and Rand DG (2022) Beliefs about COVID-19 in Canada, the United Kingdom, and the United States: A novel test of political polarization and motivated reasoning. *Personality and Social Psychology Bulletin*, 48(5), 750–765. https://doi.org/10.1177/01461672211023652.

Pigden C (2019) Popper revisited, or what is wrong with conspiracy theories? In Coady D (ed.), *Conspiracy theories.* Routledge, 17–43.

Pillay N (2020). Kinship capital: young mothers, kinship networks and support in urban South Africa. *Social Dynamics*, 46(2), 185–203. https://doi.org/10.1080/02533952.2020.1804120.

Pipes D (1999) *Conspiracy: How the paranoid style flourishes and where it comes from.* Simon and Schuster.

Pollock G, Brock T and Ellison M (2015) Populism, ideology and contradiction: Mapping young people's political views. *The Sociological Review* 63, 141–166.

Popoli G and Longus A (2021) Gender differences and the five facets of conspiracy theory. *International Journal of Psychological Studies* 13(3), 64–69.

Post W (2020) Opinion | After the Beirut explosion, enough is enough. This government must go. In YouTube.

Prior M, Sood G and Khanna K (2015) You cannot be serious: The impact of accuracy incentives on partisan bias in reports of economic perceptions. *Quarterly Journal of Political Science* 10(4), 489–518.

Proudfoot P (2022) Conspiracy, sectarianism, and the failure of the uprising. In Proudfoot P (ed.), *Rebel populism*. Manchester University Press, 173–197.

Räikkä J (2009) On political conspiracy theories. *Journal of Political Philosophy* 17(2), 185–201.

Ramos MdM, Machado RdO and Cerqueira-Santos E (2022) "It's true! I saw it on WhatsApp": Social media, covid-19, and political-ideological orientation in Brazil. *Trends in Psychology* 30(3), 570–590.

Rathje J (2021) For Reich and Volksgemeinschaft – Against the world conspiracy: Antisemitism and sovereignism in the Federal Republic of Germany since 1945. *Antisemitism Studies* 5(1), 100–138.

Reuters (2022) Trudeau's Joke about Paying Media Is Taken Out of context. www.reuters.com/article/idUSL1N2UE2UC/ (accessed January 29, 2024).

Robinson L (2021) Canaries in the climate coal mine: Climate change and COVID-19 as meta-crisis. *First Monday* 26(11), https://doi.org/10.5210/fm .v26i11.12356.

Roets A and Van Hiel A (2011) Item selection and validation of a brief, 15-item version of the need for closure scale. *Personality and Individual Differences* 50(1), 90–94.

Romer D and Jamieson KH (2020) Conspiracy theories as barriers to controlling the spread of COVID-19 in the US. *Social Science & Medicine* 263, 113356.

Roose K (2021) What Is QAnon, the Viral Pro-Trump Conspiracy Theory. *The New York Times* 3.

Rosenberg M (1965) Rosenberg self-esteem scale. *Journal of Religion and Health*.

Roslington J (2014) "England is fighting us everywhere": Geopolitics and conspiracy thinking in wartime Morocco. *The Journal of North African Studies* 19(4), 501–517.

Salles D, de Medeiros PM, Santini RM and Barros CE (2023) The far-right smokescreen: Environmental conspiracy and culture wars on Brazilian YouTube. *Social Media+ Society* 9(3), 20563051231196876.

Santini RM, Salles D and Barros CE (2022) We love to hate George Soros: A cross-platform analysis of the globalism conspiracy theory campaign in Brazil. *Convergence* 28(4), 983–1006.

Sarathchandra D and Haltinner K (2021) How believing climate change is a "hoax" shapes climate skepticism in the United States. *Environmental Sociology* 7(3), 225–238.

Schlipphak B, Isani M and Back MD (2022) Conspiracy theory beliefs and political trust: The moderating role of political communication. *Politics and Governance* 10(4), 157–167.

Shin I, Wang L and Lu Y-T (2022) Twitter and endorsed (fake) news: The influence of endorsement by strong ties, celebrities, and a user majority on credibility of fake news during the COVID-19 pandemic. *International Journal of Communication* 16, 23.

Siddiqui N (2020) Who do you believe? Political parties and conspiracy theories in Pakistan. *Party Politics* 26(2), 107–119.

Silva HM (2022) Information and misinformation about climate change: Lessons from Brazil. *Ethics in Science and Environmental Politics* 22, 51–56.

Smallpage SM, Enders AM, Drochon H and Uscinski JE (2023) The impact of social desirability bias on conspiracy belief measurement across cultures. *Political Science Research and Methods* 11(3), 555–569.

Snyder A (2017) *Jews don't need Jesus … and other misconceptions: Reflections of a Jewish believer.* Moody.

Soares FB, Recuero R, Volcan T, Fagundes G and Sodré G (2021) Research note: Bolsonaro's firehose: How Covid-19 disinformation on WhatsApp was used to fight a government political crisis in Brazil. *The Harvard Kennedy School Misinformation Review* 2(1), 1–13.

Spring M (2020) Beirut Explosion: How Conspiracy Theories Spread on Social Media. www.bbc.com/news/53669029 (accessed January 30, 2024).

Šrol J, Ballová Mikušková E and Čavojová V (2021) When we are worried, what are we thinking? Anxiety, lack of control, and conspiracy beliefs amidst the COVID-19 pandemic. *Applied Cognitive Psychology* 35(3), 720–729.

Stauffer V (2006) *The Bavarian Illuminati in America: The New England conspiracy scare, 1798.* Courier Corporation.

Stecula DA and Pickup M (2021) Social media, cognitive reflection, and conspiracy beliefs. *Frontiers in Political Science* 3, 647957.

Steenberg B, Sokani A, Myburgh N, Mutevedzi P and Madhi SA (2023) COVID-19 vaccination rollout: Aspects of hesitancy in South Africa. *Vaccines* 11(2), 407.

Stockemer D (2023) Conspiracy theories in the US: Who believes in them? *The Forum*. 21(4), 529–550. https://doi.org/10.1515/for-2023-2022.

Stockemer D and Bordeleau J-N (2024). Conspiracy theories and their believers in an era of misinformation. *Harvard Kennedy School (HKS) Misinformation Review* 5(6): https://misinforeview.hks.harvard.edu/article/conspiracy-theor ies-and-their-believers-in-an-era-of-misinformation/.

Sullivan M (2014) Hezbollah in Syria: Institute for the Study of War. www.jstor .org/stable/resrep07896 (accessed February 26, 2024).

Swami V, Voracek M, Stieger S, Tran US and Furnham A (2014) Analytic thinking reduces belief in conspiracy theories. *Cognition* 133(3), 572–585.

Szwako J (2023) Négationnisme, antimondialisme et défense de la liberté dans le «réactionnarisme» brésilien contemporain. *Brésil (s). Sciences Humaines et Sociales* (23). https://doi.org/10.4000/bresils.15071

Thompson JD (2019) Predatory schools and student non-lives: A discourse analysis of the Safe Schools Coalition Australia controversy. *Sex Education* 19(1), 41–53.

Thórisdóttir H, Mari S and Krouwel A (2020) Conspiracy theories, political ideology and political behaviour. In Butter M, Knight P (eds.), *Routledge handbook of conspiracy theories*. Routledge, 304–316.

Tollefson J (2021) How Trump turned conspiracy theory research upside down. *Nature* 590, 192–193.

Travica B (2022) COVID-19 conspiracy theories in Canada: Evidence, verifi- cation, and implications for decision making. *Journal of Economics and Management* 44(1), 236–265.

Ullah I, Khan KS, Tahir MJ, Ahmed A and Harapan H (2021) Myths and conspiracy theories on vaccines and COVID-19: Potential effect on global vaccine refusals. *Vacunas* 22(2), 93–97.

Umam A, Muluk H and Milla M (2018) The need for cognitive closure and belief in conspiracy theories: An exploration of the role of religious funda- mentalism in cognition. In Ariyanto AA, Muluk H, Newcombe P, et al. (eds.), *Diversity in unity: Perspectives from psychology and behavioral sciences*, Routledge/Taylor & Francis Group, 629–637. https://doi.org/10.1201/ 9781315225302-79.

UNAIDS (2022) South Africa: Country Fact Sheet. www.unaids.org/en/region scountries/countries/southafrica (accessed October 23, 2023).

Uscinski J, Enders AM, Klofstad C and Stoler J (2022) Cause and effect: On the antecedents and consequences of conspiracy theory beliefs. *Current Opinion in Psychology* 47, 101364.

Uscinski JE (2018) The study of conspiracy theories. *Argumenta* 3(2), 233–245.

Uscinski JE, Enders AM, Klofstad C et al. (2020) Why do people believe COVID-19 conspiracy theories? *Harvard Kennedy School Misinformation Review* 1(3), 1–12.

Uscinski JE and Parent JM (2014) *American conspiracy theories*. Oxford University Press.

van Prooijen J-W, Amodio DM, Boot A et al. (2022) A longitudinal analysis of conspiracy beliefs and Covid-19 health responses. *Psychological Medicine*, 53(12), 5709–5716, https://doi.org/10.1017/S0033291722002938.

Van Prooijen J-W and Douglas KM (2017) Conspiracy theories as part of history: The role of societal crisis situations. *Memory Studies* 10(3), 323–333.

van Prooijen J-W (2017) Why education predicts decreased belief in conspiracy theories. *Applied Cognitive Psychology* 31(1), 50–58.

Vegetti F and Littvay L (2022) Belief in conspiracy theories and attitudes toward political violence. *Italian Political Science Review/Rivista Italiana di Scienza Politica* 52(1), 18–32.

Walter AS and Drochon H (2022) Conspiracy thinking in Europe and America: A comparative study. *Political Studies* 70(2), 483–501.

Winston AS (2021) "Jews will not replace us!": Antisemitism, interbreeding and immigration in historical context. *American Jewish History* 105(1), 1–24.

Wood MJ, Douglas KM and Sutton RM (2012) Dead and alive: Beliefs in contradictory conspiracy theories. *Social Psychological and Personality Science* 3(6), 767–773.

Zadrozny B and Collins B (2018) NBC News. https://paulfurber.net/nbc/gmail-nbcnews.pdf.

Zag H and Mifdal M (2024) Polarized framing of scientific uncertainty during COVID-19 pandemic in Morocco. *Atlantic Journal of Communication*, 1–21. https://doi.org/10.1080/15456870.2024.2370274.

Zhang Y, Yue Z, Yang X, Chen F and Kwak N (2022) How a peripheral ideology becomes mainstream: Strategic performance, audience reaction, and news media amplification in the case of QAnon Twitter accounts. *New Media & Society*, 26(10), 5597–5618. 14614448221137324.

Zihiri S, Lima G, Han J, Cha M and Lee W (2022) QAnon shifts into the mainstream, remains a far-right ally. *Heliyon* 8(2), 1–7.

Acknowledgments

We would like to express our gratitude to the Konrad Adenauer Stiftung Canada for their ongoing financial support throughout this project. Portions of the material in this Element were presented at the *Comparative Conspiracy Theory Workshop* held in September 2023 at the University of Ottawa as well as at the *2023 World Congress of the International Political Science Association* in Buenos Aires, Argentina. We appreciate the valuable feedback and suggestions from the participants at these events. Our heartfelt thanks also go to our outstanding team of research assistants – Danika Brown, Acadia Gilchrist, Timothy Gulliver, Grace Hobson, Alice Prindiville-Porto, and Lina Tahir – for their invaluable contributions to this project.

Cambridge Elements ≡

Comparative Political Behavior

Raymond Duch
University of Oxford

Raymond Duch is the co-founder and Director of the Centre for Experimental Social Sciences (CESS) at Nuffield College University of Oxford. He established and directed similar CESS centers in Chile, China, and India. He is also co-Director of the Candour Project that assembles a global team of research scholars with expertise in behavioral economics and data analytics addressing challenging health policy issues.

Anja Neundorf
University of Glasgow

Anja Neundorf is a Professor of Politics and Research Methods at the School of Social and Political Sciences at the University of Glasgow, UK. Before joining Glasgow, she held positions at the University of Nottingham (2013–2019) and Nuffield College, University of Oxford (2010–2012). She received her PhD from the University of Essex.

Randy Stevenson
Rice University

Randolph Stevenson is the Radoslav Tsanoff Professor of Public Affairs at Rice University in Houston, Texas. Professor Stevenson works and teaches in the areas of survey design, applied statistical methods, comparative mass political behavior, comparative political psychology, and experimental design.

About the Series

This Elements series is aimed at students and researchers interested in understanding how and why the political behaviour, perceptions, attitudes, emotional responses, interest, knowledge, and identities of citizens are conditioned on the political, social, and economic contexts in which they experience the political world.

Cambridge Elements ≡

Comparative Political Behavior

Elements in the Series

Printed in the United States
by Baker & Taylor Publisher Services